Praise

'Affectingly personal, achingly earnest, and something close to necessary.' *Vogue*

'An important book about all of the latest cultural issues everyone is arguing over – from #MeToo and privilege to free speech and identity politics . . . Really well done.' *The Saturday Post*

'Personal, convincing, unflinching.' *Tablet*

'An elegantly-composed treatise against tribalism and cancel culture that seamlessly weaves in personal anecdotes.' *Elle*

'Daum's writing is brave and engaging; she does some hard thinking about our times and demands that we do too.' *Newsweek*

'A book of thoughtful, provocative essays on everything from the Trump presidency to identity politics to generational differences and beyond. At a time when nuance of any kind is often dismissed, Daum offers thoughtful takes on hot-button topics.' *New York Post*

'This book is the eloquent testament of a card-carrying feminist who abhors the stranglehold that political correctness has placed on intellectual life in America. As such, it is to be applauded – and I do.' Vivian Gornick

'Sharp, brazen, and undeniably controversial.' *Kirkus*

'Daum, an old-school essayist more in the vein of Joan Didion and Nora Ephron than xoJane and Jezebel, says she will continue to tease out the nuances that exist all around us, even as doing so becomes increasingly . . . problematic.' *The Stranger*

Praise for *The Unspeakable*

'A fantastic collection of essays: funny, clever, and moving (often at the same time), never more universal than in its most personal moments (in other words, throughout), and written with enviable subtlety, precision, and spring.' Geoff Dyer

'I loved these essays for a completely startling reason: they give voice and shape to so many of my own muddled thoughts – and to lurking sentiments I've never looked square in the face.' Julia Glass

'*The Unspeakable* speaks with wit and warmth and artful candor, the fruits of an exuberant and consistently surprising intelligence. These are essays that dig under the surface of what we might expect to feel in order to discover what we actually feel instead. I was utterly captivated by Meghan Daum's sensitive fidelity to the complexity of lived experience.' Leslie Jamison

'[*The Unspeakable*] is formidable, lucid, and persuasive. Daum writes with confidence and an elegant defiance of expectation . . . I would follow her words anywhere.' *The New York Times Book Review*

'Sharp, witty and illuminating, Daum's essays offer refreshing insight into the complexities of living an examined life in a world hostile to the multifaceted face of truth. An honest and humorously edgy collection.' *Kirkus*

'I think it's fair to say that I can't tell you what Meghan Daum's remarkable book means to me – the exceptional often denies verbalization. Her diverse subject matter aside – Mom, Joni Mitchell, the fetishization of food – it's Daum's galvanizing energy that one finds so attractive.' Hilton Als

Praise for *My Misspent Youth*

'An empathetic reporter and a provocative autobiographer . . .
I finished it in a single afternoon, mesmerized and sputtering.'
Caleb Crain, *The Nation*

'Even when she's being funny, [Daum's] writing has a clarity
and intensity that just makes you feel awake.' Ira Glass

'Meghan Daum is not an eccentric exhibitionist or a self-
indulgent memoirist. Her world is suburban New Jersey girl-
hood, Vassar, publishing, and the disillusionment that results
when the reality of one's life falls short of expectations. Daum
approaches the first lesson of adulthood – that the prosaic
will intrude on the fantastic every time – without ever dis-
solving into cynicism.' *The New York Times Book Review*

'People I know still talk about Meghan Daum's 2001 debut
essay collection, *My Misspent Youth*. Nobody writing about
her generation was more incisive or entertaining than she.'
Sigrid Nunez

Praise for *Life Would Be Perfect if I Lived in That House*

'Daum has a rare gift in her ability to keep readers laughing
through her own tears.' *The New York Times Book Review*

'Like having a long, glorious, no-holds-barred conversation
with your smartest, funniest friend about all the juicy topics: real estate, class envy, bad dates, family identity, and the
discrepancies between the lives we aspire to and the lives we
lead.' Curtis Sittenfeld

'A delightful dissection of the real estate obsession that's a
hallmark of our age, recession or no.' *O, The Oprah Magazine*

'Self-deprecatingly funny . . . Daum uses her lifelong obsession with finding the ideal living space to probe domestic desire, a deeper restlessness than the search for quick profits.' *Wall Street Journal*

'Honest and endearing . . . richly drawn. . . . Daum captures the now-gone moment when real estate became a national obsession, chronicling the shared madness of those who could only take breaks from watching HGTV to discuss closing costs.' *Los Angeles Times Book Review*

'Suffused with humor and desire . . . Alternately whimsical, philosophical and psychologically probing . . . [An] enchanting, compelling memoir on the impossibility of resisting an irresistible object of desire.' *Miami Herald*

'It's a pleasure to read this author as she revisits comic misadventures and wrangles with a hot-button topic.' *Time Out New York*

'Vividly described . . . Daum exposes the modern real-estatemad female underground, where open houses (visited in rabid two-women teams) are a seasonal blood sport, Zillow is a verb, and where remodeling a collapsing farmhouse into a writer's retreat could instantly, we imagine, transform us into the George Plimpton of the prairie.' *Atlantic Monthly*

'Timely . . . Daum [is] a fine writer – candid, reflective, stylish, fun and a bit prickly. Throughout the book, she offers an unflinching portrayal of her anxieties and her aspirations.' *Associated Press*

Notting Hill Editions is an independent British publisher. The company was founded by Tom Kremer (1930–2017), champion of innovation and the man responsible for popularising the Rubik's Cube.

After a successful business career in toy invention Tom decided, at the age of eighty, to fulfil his passion for literature. In a fast-moving digital world Tom's aim was to revive the art of the essay, and to create exceptionally beautiful books that would be cherished.

Hailed as 'the shape of things to come', the family-run press brings to print the most surprising thinkers of past and present. In an era of information-overload, these collectible pocket-size books distil ideas that linger in the mind.

THE CATASTROPHE HOUR

Selected Essays

–

Meghan Daum

nh Notting Hill Editions

Published in 2025
by Notting Hill Editions Ltd
Mirefoot, Burneside, Kendal LA8 9AB

Cover design: Tom Etherington

Typeset by CB Editions, London
Printed and bound in the UK by Short Run Press

The publishers gratefully acknowledge the permission granted to
reproduce copyright material in this book. Every effort has been made
to trace and contact copyright holders and to obtain their permission
for the use of copyright material. The publisher apologises for any
errors or omissions and would be grateful if notified of any corrections
that should be incorporated in future reprints or editions of this book.

A CIP record for this book is available from the British Library.

ISBN 978-1-912559-68-8

nottinghilleditions.com

Contents

– Introduction –

xi

– The Broken-In World –

1

– Same Life, Higher Rent –

11

– Basically Dead –

22

– Species Of Grief –

30

– Playlist Of Tears –

39

– The Unbearable Halfness Of Being–

46

– 70 Million Songs –

61

– Independent Creator –

68

– What I Have In Common
With Trans Activists –

75

– Problematized –

83

– A Handsome Woman –

89

– Femcel Cope (A Case Against Early Marriage) –

100

– The Catastrophe Hour –

132

– The End Of The Personal –

156

– Acknowledgements –

171

– Introduction –

For the last five or six years, on many afternoons around 4 or 5 p.m., I've been overcome by the feeling that my life is effectively over. This is not a sense that the world is ending, which has been in vogue for quite some time now, and maybe for good reason. It's a personal forboding, a distinct feeling of being at the end of my days. My time, while technically not 'up', is disappearing in the rearview mirror. The fact that this feeling of ambient doom tends to coincide with the blue-tinged, pre-gloaming light of the late afternoon lends the whole thing a cosmic beauty, as devastating as it is awe-inspiring. As such, I've dubbed this the catastrophe hour.

Getting older is the oldest story in the world, of course. Still, the time – my time – is disappearing at a pace that is faster than I had ever anticipated and, I daresay, faster than the pace experienced by any previous generation. As far as cultural relevance goes, GenX is shaping up to have a tragically short lifespan. Just as we were finding our footing in the early to mid-2000s, getting real jobs and looking almost like respectable grownups, the twin forces of hyperspeed tech advancement and head-spinning social changes came along and fermented us before we'd even ripened on the vine. By the time we were fifty, many of us were as good as eighty. Or so it often feels to me.

The consolations of aging have always been in the eye of the beholder. Virginia Woolf, at fifty, wrote in her diaries of feeling 'poised to shoot forth quite free straight and undeflected my bolts whatever they are.' She did not believe in aging, she said, but rather 'forever altering one's aspect to the sun.' I am now three years past the age Woolf was when she talked about altering her aspect to the sun. And while I don't know enough about astrology to connect the dots of my memories to trail markers of the earth's orbit, I've lately become aware of a sort of baseline visceral sensation hovering over my emotional life. Again and again, this sensation conjures the same sentiment: I'm glad I lived when I did. Specifically, I'm glad I was young when I was.

Life to me these days often feels like I'm backing up slowly from a tense and increasingly untenable situation. If the world in the post-Trump, post-George Floyd, post-COVID, post-whatever-happened-five-minutes-ago age feels in many ways like a bank robbery in progress, I'm the lady who was finishing up with the teller at precisely the moment the robbers entered the building. While the rest of the customers dropped to the ground, I managed to slither away just in time, my transaction completed, the door hitting me firmly but not violently on the way out.

Safely outside, I can peer through the glass as the people younger than I surrender like hostages to the demands and punishments of the digital era. Fledgling journalists churn out multiple articles per day for a fraction of what I was paid twenty years ago (and are appraised not by the quality of their work but by the quantity of their clicks). Artists forge their own lonely and starving paths, unsupported by institutions and economies that once upon a time, for better or worse, buoyed them enough to at least keep them paddling along. Teenagers with undeveloped frontal lobes are effectively subject to twenty-four-hour social media surveillance, their every poor choice and dumbass move recorded for potentially cataclysmic posterity.

There are things I did and said as a teenager that would ruin me today if they had been captured, immortalized and weaponized per the current protocol. I'd give you some hints as to what these things might be but, honestly, I cannot remember. In shame or mortification or unconscious self-protection I've blocked them out. I have sense memories of these idiocies, but there's no precision to them. They remain preserved in an impressionistic muck. In turn, that muck is what preserves my ability to live with myself. How lucky to have lived in a time of such muck. How lucky to have grown up in private.

The essays in this collection were written, for the most part, between 2017 and 2024. The subjects covered include divorce, travel, dating, music, friendship, beauty, aging, death, art, solitude, music, money and real estate. (I could go on, but I'll stop at real estate, where the buck always stops.) Though many were written during the Trump administration and into the pandemic era, I'm relieved to tell you that they don't linger on politics or Covid.

It feels important to say these essays were written in the privacy of my own mind. By that I mean they did not germinate in tweets or blog posts or Instagram stories. They are not my 'take' on anything. Instead, they are products of those tender, fleeting moments when a writer finds herself staring into space (or out her window, or at the wall) and thinking about what she wants to say not to her social media followers but to her reader. They were inspired not by news headlines or social media dustups but by the free-floating anxiety that underscores and perpetuates all of that. They are my attempt to grab some emotional abstractions out of the air and examine them until they can start to make sense. They're about the pleasures of staring out the window or even staring at the wall.

The final three essays in this collection are brand new; you are reading them here for the first time. Others appeared on the platform *Medium*, specifically the no-longer-extant publication *GEN*, where I wrote a regular, magazine-style column (with real editors; a rare luxury today) that lived a rather shadowy life behind a paywall. Others lived in my proverbial desk drawer and some, more recently, have assumed a place behind that paywall *du jour* known as my Substack page. I have arranged them in chronological order by date, starting with the earliest and ending with the three new ones, written in 2024.

The best-known invocation of the word catastrophe might come from *Zorba The Greek*, the 1946 novel made into the 1964 film starring Anthony Quinn. Asked by a stranger if he's a married man, the exuberant, perennially exasperated protagonist replies 'Yes, I'm married. Wife, children, house. The full catastrophe.'

The last phrase proved resonant enough to become the title of a novel and at least one self-help book, not to mention a John Cougar Mellencamp song.

Say you have no wife or are not a wife yourself. Say you have neither children nor a house. Is that a double catastrophe? Or a tragic absense of catastrophe? Is it obscene to claim castastrophe for private use? This is a word that describes wars and devastating floods and fires. Are the vicissitudes of any given life worthy of such, well . . . catastrophizing? These essays are an attempt to answer, or at least entertain, that question. And even if the question is ultimately unanswerable, my hope is that by gathering them into a book they will find themselves in conversation, maybe even occasionally arguments, with one another.

Finally, I will say this: There are those who say that books hardly matter anymore. They say the printed page is dead and that assigning any value to books as physical objects is the hallmark of a person who is himself on the cusp of extinction. (I suggest as much in the final essay, but don't skip ahead.) However, I became a writer because I believe words deserve space in the physical world. That is how you prevent them from becoming extinct. I write books because I believe committing words to the page is as sacred a vow as there is. And though these essays were born in the era of SEO-friendly titles and page view analytics (in *Medium*, readers were told exactly how many minutes it would take them to read each one; I'll spare you those calculations) I still think their true home is between two covers that can be held by human hands. Insofar as that particular experience may be in its final hours, it is my honor to place these pages before you. In the event of a real catastrophe, you can always burn them with firewood.

– The Broken-In World –

September 2016

At the age of forty-five, I found myself in the surprisingly unsurprising situation of filing for divorce. To be accurate, I was the respondent in this filing, a decision based solely upon the fact that my husband was remaining in our home state of California while I was taking one of our two giant dogs and driving to New York City in order to 'restart my life'. (A somewhat ironic notion since, many years earlier, I'd attempted to restart my life by making the same move in the opposite direction. But what is the human condition if not a perpetually indecisive toggle switch?)

Even though it made more sense for my husband to file for divorce against me rather than the other way around, there was no wronged party here. There was no measurable infidelity or betrayal, just your standard irreconcilable differences, a phrase I've come to believe is legal jargon for 'can no longer ride in the car together due to frequency of arguments about the driver's braking skills, texting proclivities and degree of willingness to make left turns into busy intersections.' If I was really forced to get specific about our particular brand of irreconcilable differences, I'd have

1

to say they were both as petty as my refusing to sing along when my husband played Neil Young songs on the guitar and as monumental as facing up to the fact that I'm infinitely happier and less insane when I live alone (or possibly with a roommate who travels frequently) than am I when I live even with the person I love and care about most.

And so there you have it. Divorced. Or at least well on the way to it. As any divorced person knows, which I guess is to say, 'as about half of all adults know or will eventually know', much of the battle is going public with it. Sure, your close friends won't be surprised: they've been hearing you whine for years now, it's the people in the outer rings who will be shocked; the workplace colleagues and the casual acquaintances and the housekeeper. (Though who are we kidding? The housekeeper knew before anyone.) Those who belong to the divorce club will respond appropriately. Their sympathy will be imbued with solidarity. Their condolences will carry a strong whiff of congratulations.

Others will cover their mouths and gasp with a jolt, as though they just happened to glance out their window and witness a plane crash. They'll cluck their tongues and cock their heads. They'll reach out to you as if consoling a crying child. And though they will have only the best of intentions, these gestures will just make you feel worse. They will make you feel sadder than you already were in that moment. They will make

2

you say to yourself, here I was, having a perfectly normal conversation and not feeling devastated about my divorce and this person just reminded me to be devastated all over again.

But after a while of this, these gestures will begin to make you smile ever so slightly. You will see that gestures will be in vain, they are the domain of the well-meaning but uninitiated. That is because a person getting a divorce is the opposite of a crying child. A person getting a divorce is an adult who has decided to set a quit date for the misery and crying. It is a person who has chosen pain over ambivalence and learned one of the great lessons of life, which is that ambivalence is the worst pain there is.

Yet people fear divorce the way they fear illness. They look away when they see it in others. They search for evidence of weakness, of moral deficiency, of crimes they can't imagine committing themselves. They tell themselves that given enough healthy life choices it's possible to lower their odds into, if not negligibility, at least something that will, if it should ever come to that, feel more like a force majeure than the real statistical possibility everyone knows it is.

I can't say I got married thinking I'd eventually get divorced (though I know a few who have) but if you had told me that almost exactly seven years to the day that I stood in a white lace dress and almost floor-length veil (that veil was and remains the most exhilarating garment I've ever attached to my body) I'd be

3

receiving a 'dissolution notice' from the state of California I wouldn't exactly have fallen out of my chair. Marriage had never been an abiding goal of mine. Practice serial monogamy well into your thirties and you've got enough pretend little simulated-marriages under your belt that the real thing loses some of its mystique.

Still, I went through my twenties and most of my thirties wrestling with the internalized and not-always-entirely-conscious pressure that all but the most wild-spirited young people operate under: the assumption that my social life was essentially a vehicle for finding one singularly qualified person with whom I could enact some version of settling down. I made quite a big deal of saying I was on no such search. I liked to think of myself as, if not exactly wild-spirited, than wild-spirit adjacent in some manner. But the truth is that I bought into the idea of legally sanctioned, lifelong monogamy as earnestly as anyone else. And as much as I could see that it was a big gamble no matter how you played it, I thought that waiting as long as possible to marry constituted a sort of inoculation against divorce. Not in the 'couples who delay marriage have higher success rates' sense (in fact, those success rates begin to reverse once you reach your mid-thirties) but in the sense that I thought that waiting until we were older meant we'd have less time to grow tired of one another. A lot of the people I saw divorcing had been in the saddle together for decades. They had kids leaving home, mortgages paid off, last gasps of sexual vitality begging not to be squandered. By the time my husband and I reached the twenty-year mark, we'd be too old to bother splitting up. We'd be sixty, which seemed to me at forty less like actual life but a grayed-out silhouette of life.

It had only taken me until forty-six to see the folly in that, to understand that the seeds of sixty, planted at birth, are saplings at twenty and by the mid-forties have grown into giant, flapping fronds of inchoate physicality. Desiccated on the edges but coursing with some mysterious something in the veins (blood? water? the collective tears of a lifetime?), middle-aged carnal desire is a sweet, capricious beast. It's a desire that sometimes feels less rooted in abject carnality than in plain interest.

To witness two people of a certain age getting to know one another in a way that might lead to physical intimacy is to see anthropology in action. There is social theory happening here, urban planning, case studies in family law. There is history meeting history. There is baggage being lifted off a carousel and introduced like dogs sniffing each other on the sidewalk. There is no pretense of freshness, of blamelessness, of idealizing or being idealized. Coyness, too, seems in the wrong key. First dates cut right to the chase. The real stuff gets trotted out right away: the custody arrangements, the miscarriages, the mortgage payments, the therapy sessions. Instead of talking about the best concert you ever saw you talk about the day you realized your previous life was going to be just that, a previous life from which only a few residual threads now hang from your shirtsleeves. This is now the story you trot out when you want to signal that you might be willing to let yourself be known.

This is the story of how you broke yourself, of how your world sprung a crack right underneath where you were standing. And as your story joins the chorus of stories being told and listened to in as many versions as there are broken people to tell and hear them, you slide into a new kind of world. It's a world in which the stiff hide of convention and expectation has softened into supple leather. It's a world that can no longer support pretense, a world where those Facebook posts advertising marital bliss are confirmed as the bullshit we always deep down knew them to be. It's a world built on scar tissue, which turns out to be a surprisingly solid foundation. And at some point, without quite realizing it, your life goes from broken to broken in.

It turns out this is something of a magical place. Like a Narnia for disaffected adults, the broken-in world comes with its share of strange, terrifying creatures but ultimately procures a kind of divine comfort. During the first few months that I permanently separated from my husband, I found myself on the receiving end of dozens of domestic war stories. Friends I hadn't seen for a decade or more, whose apparently untarnished lives I'd followed on Facebook with a mixture of envy and genuine happiness for their good fortune, were suddenly wanting to get together and tell me how it really was. Having heard about my 'situation', they were compelled to tell me about the affairs and financial transgressions and mental health issues and slightly fucked up, less-than-totally-existentially-fulfilling children that now filled the void of their still-discontented lives.

People I'd long considered pillars of decency and in some cases major geeks turned out to have been shouting at each other in their kitchens in front of their kids, in their driveways in front of their neighbors, in the offices of therapists and lawyers. They were sleeping with old flames at college reunions, keeping secret Tinder accounts, keeping secret bank accounts, developing gambling addictions, drinking too much, hating their jobs, hating their lives, hating themselves. It was horrifying.

It was fantastic. I couldn't get enough. I sat with them for hours, nodding in sympathy, shaking my head in empathy. It wasn't that I took pleasure in their suffering. If I'd had the power, I would have whisked any of them back into their fantasyland of their Facebook personae – for their kids' sake if not their own. (Though that's a reflexive bit of sentimentality; anyone who ever thought they were preserving their children's innocence by enlisting them in the project of impersonating a happy family is engaged in a level of denial that borders on cruelty.) The truth was that I loved this world that we'd entered. I loved the broken-in world. I loved it because it felt like honest living, the sort of emotional equivalent to working with your hands. Everyone should do such work at least once in their lives. How could I have known I would take so well to the emotional equivalent of manual labor? How could I have known that my most satisfying life was a broken life?

When I got to New York, I moved first to Brooklyn. That is what you do now when you move to New York. I can't remember hating a place more. I lived in fancy Brooklyn, which is to say a part of Brooklyn that had seemed intractably crime ridden when I'd last lived in New York twenty years earlier but was now a glorified suburb; Connecticut for people who would never move to Connecticut. High-grade strollers choked the narrow sidewalks, having long displaced the residents of the old neighborhood. Moms strode about in yoga pants, dads did self-congratulating drop-offs at the 'good public school' before boarding the F-train to their midtown offices.

I couldn't figure out why I was so miserable here, why I felt like a member of another species. Was it nothing more than the ache of divorce? The alternating shock and relief of aloneness? Or was it that my neighbors, with their young marriages and younger children and determination to keep the whole enviable shebang intact, were not yet broken? They were leather as stiff as a shiny purse. Their baggage was still being assembled and packed. It wasn't scuffed and distressed and strewn all around them like mine was. It would be someday, but it wasn't yet.

Eventually I gave up and moved with my Saint Bernard to Manhattan, into a clanking old building on the northern banks of the Hudson River where the wind howled mercilessly through the airshaft and the elevator broke constantly. It was a building where so many people lived alone that it was not infrequent that someone would drop dead in his or her apartment, only to be found days later after the neighbors noticed a smell. Whenever this happened, a little memorial with a photo and flowers was placed in the lobby. Evidently, a woman who had lived in my apartment years earlier had fallen to the ground, died suddenly of a heart attack and gone unnoticed for so long that the bedroom floor was so damaged that it had to be replaced.

'But don't worry,' said Lois, my kind, seventy-year-old next-door neighbor. 'That won't happen to you. If you dropped dead your dog would bark.'

Another neighbor, Marlene, was seventy-five and we sometimes met for coffee in the cafe around the corner. Marlene was divorced, had never had children and had recently moved with her dog from Los Angeles to New York, where she shared a large apartment in our building with her harpsichord teacher. One afternoon I found Marlene sitting in the lobby with her dog, flipping through the *New York Times* but looking visibly shaken. She told me she was waiting for her ex-husband, whom she hadn't seen in two years but was finally making good on their divorce agreement allowing him to visit the dog. He had flown all the way to New York in order to walk the dog around the block and then bring it back. 'I told him it was supposed to rain,' she said. 'But he's determined to come anyway. He may do it again tomorrow before he goes back.'

The next day, while walking my dog by the river, I saw Marlene's dog with a man I assumed to be the ex-husband. He was tall yet stooped, graying but also gray in posture and in bearing. He wore a fishing hat and a too-thin jacket, as Californians do. I watched him gazing out at the Hudson as the dog sniffed the banks. He had flown 3,000 miles to spend half an hour staring across the water at New Jersey, probably wondering if his dog even remembered him. The river that day was brackish yet choppy. It struck me in that moment as a vast sea of sadness, a tattered artery breaking the land in two emphatically distinct pieces. It was devastating. It was beautiful. I couldn't get enough. It was broken. I was home.

– Same Life, Higher Rent –

June 2017

F riday evening, 8 p.m., early summer, New York City. I sit at my desk, face aglow in Macintosh luminescence. On the desk sits the detritus of the hour, of the day, the week, the season. There is dinner of sushi in the little takeout tray from the supermarket. There is leftover coffee in a mug from the afternoon. There are books and notebooks and checkbooks. There are pens and lip balms and hair ties and postage stamps and unmatched earrings and a Metro-Card. There are a gazillion paper napkins for some reason. There is a computer modem whose lights flash with the irregular, listing cadence of a heart murmur. There are several Word documents up on that glowing screen, each competing for attention, not so much with one another, but with the email interface to which all roads lead back.

It is 1997. It is 2017. It doesn't matter. It is both. In twenty years, my life has come full circle, 360 degrees for real. People often say 360 degrees when they mean 180. They say full circle when they're really talking about a semicircle. It's an oddly human error, as though they can't quite grasp the concept of a human being turning on an axis as readily as the earth itself.

But in my case, it's true. At forty-seven, my life looks uncannily the same way it did at twenty-seven.

How did I get here? Nearly two decades ago, I moved from New York City to the Midwest and then to California, where I came as close to settling down as I'm probably ever going to come, which is to say I got married. Nearly two years ago, the marriage ended, and I got in the car and literally drove through my life in reverse. I drove west to east, backward in time, until I landed right back where I started: alone in a scuff-marked apartment in a clanking old Manhattan building much like the one I occupied in my twenties, eating supermarket sushi at my desk and trying mightily (yes, on a Friday evening) to complete a writing assignment that was due the week before.

There are a few differences, but they are minor. Because it is 2017 and not 1997, I am writing on a Mac-Book Air laptop and not a Quadra 650. The modem is wireless rather than dial-up, which means email comes in automatically and my opportunities for screen-based distraction and procrastination exceed anything I could have imagined back then. Thanks to these opportunities, I estimate that my attention span in 2017 is about 30 percent of what it was in 1997. Conversely, my rent back then was 30 percent of what it is now.

Same life, higher rent. This could be the motto of my life after forty-five. For many years, I had a very different life. I had what is commonly perceived of as a grown-up life, with a husband and a mortgage and a yard that required regular upkeep. There is much to be said for this life. For starters, it's a lucky thing to find someone you like enough to enlist as a partner for such an endeavor. There's also no getting around the fact that the gears of the daily grind tend to run smoother when they're greased with the benefits of coupledom. You never quite realize what a pain it is to drive yourself to every social event you attend until you have someone to share the burden with you. (Second glass of wine? Sure!) You never quite realize how much food you've got sitting around on high pantry shelves until there's someone who can reach it for you – and, in my case, cook it for you.

But even my 1997 self would have told you that the membership associated with these benefits probably wasn't going to be a lifetime deal. My 1997 self would have suspected, correctly, that such benefits would lead to a severe enough case of impostor syndrome that I would slowly, and very sadly, wend my way back to the life I had before. What I would not have understood were the ways in which this return was less a defeat than a homecoming. I did not know that the life I was living in my twenties, a life I was certain was a temporary condition, was, in fact, the only one for me.

This is not to be confused with my best life or even the life I'm still on some level programmed to believe I want. I'm talking about my situational set point, the version of myself that inevitably swings back into the foreground even if I've managed to pretend to be another kind of person for a period of time. It's like an existential version of that number on the bathroom scale that manages to own you no matter what you do. You can drift above it or claw your way below it, but eventually it's always there again.

I've spent plenty of time over the years fighting my situational set point. I've lived with boyfriends and roommates and, of course, my husband. I've attempted to keep my desk neat. I've given credence to all those studies suggesting that people who live with long-term partners are healthier and live longer than sad solo dwellers who eat while standing over the sink – or, in my case, at my desk. I've tried to stick it out. But always, I swing back. Like it or not, this life works for me. I love living alone. I love eating when and where and what I want. I love sleeping when I want and socializing when I want and being able to travel at the last minute without throwing another person's life out of whack as a result. I love talking to my friends on the phone for hours without worrying about someone in the next room overhearing me and (at least in my imagination) silently judging me for all the cackling gossip and bombastic complaining. I love hosting parties by myself. I love drinking that first cup of coffee in the morning while standing by my window and (did I mention I pay more rent now?) looking out at the barges floating by on the Hudson River.

All of that I did and also loved in my twenties. The only difference was that I didn't realize how much I loved it. Also, my window had a view of a brick wall.

I'll state the obvious and say that much, if not all, of the reason my life hasn't changed is that I'm not a parent. Children are life's great timekeepers and when you don't live with any, you're at the mercy of your own internal clock, which, like everything else in the body, becomes less reliable with age. In that sense – and probably in several other senses, but who's counting? – my life is very different than that of most women in their forties, the majority of whom share their personal space with members of future generations and therefore have no trouble distinguishing the past from the present.

If I had a kid, I trust I'd have no trouble making that distinction either. At least I hope I wouldn't, since eating packaged sushi off a desk that's covered with hair accessories is no life for a child. Neither is having a routine in which it's possible for many days to pass in which there is no need to leave the apartment. If I felt like a recluse in my twenties, I'm a bona fide shut-in now. That's because if I need food or clothing or contact lens solution, I no longer have to go to a store to buy it. I can just click 'buy now' and stay home and wait for the mail. This is a huge quality-of-life improvement over having to walk four blocks to CVS.

If the digital age has had a profound impact on my shopping habits, it's left my social life – at least its romantic iterations – surprisingly untouched. The dating patterns of my 1997 self and my 2017 self are virtually identical, which is to say they're sporadic, half-hearted and marked by an attitude that lurches between grouchy and what would now be called DGAF (for the uninitiated, that's Don't Give A Fuck, a phrase I rarely use in either long or abbreviated form). In 1997, there were only two ways you could wind up on a date: You could be fixed up by a third party, or you could happen to meet someone in real life, exchange phone numbers, make use of those numbers and have an actual voice conversation in which a date is proposed and then accepted.

Because of all that heavy lifting, it was rare to find yourself in a situation that you might construe as a date – at least for heterosexual women in my social circles, where the underrepresentation of men in general resulted in an overrepresentation of the kind of men who couldn't be bothered to ask women out. I estimate that throughout my entire twenties, I probably had fewer than twenty proper dates, by which I mean outings with men who called me on the telephone, asked me out and bought me dinner under less-than-platonic pretenses. (Going on a date is not to be conflated with having a boyfriend, the latter of which was in no way dependent on the former.) In this age of Tinder and Match.com, you can go on seven dates a week, or maybe even twice that many if you have the energy, without having to summon up any courage whatsoever. At least that's what I've heard. I'll never know, because every time I load a dating app onto my phone,

I delete it and cancel my subscription after one date. In my first two years back in New York, I joined and quit OkCupid three times and went on three dates in total.

The men were perfectly fine, some quite lovely. Still, I could never quite muster enough enthusiasm to see them again. Even though they had twenty to thirty more years' worth of things to talk about than the men I'd dated in my twenties, they were still no match for the solace of my apartment and the familiar rhythms of my own company. I couldn't imagine going home with any of them, partly because there's nothing I like more than going home by myself. If that sounds like the waning desire of a middle-aged woman, I can tell you that it's not that at all. I was the same way in my twenties.

The relationships I sought out back then were temporary by design, preferably long distance. I had a weakness for men whose unsuitability I could reframe as exoticism, men who didn't read books or who had troubling political beliefs or, best of all, lived far away and existed mainly as voices over the phone and occasional houseguests. I told myself I wanted a real boyfriend – and I often grew frustrated when these men inevitably stopped going through the motions of acting like one – but in hindsight, I can see I wanted no such thing. I wanted the safety of impermanence. I wanted round-trip excursions on ships whose pleasures were all the sweeter for my knowing that I'd eventually be returned to my home port.

When I got divorced, I thought I was entering act three of the meandering stage play of my adulthood. In this act, I thought the starting gun that I could never quite fire in my twenties would finally go off in my forties, sending me sprinting into a glorious, fully self-actualized future like some kind of nervous but nimble gazelle. I'd have the wind at my back, yet it would also be blowing gently into my face so that my hair looked amazing. I didn't turn out to be entirely wrong about this. By any objective measure, I'm doing better now than I did back then. My career is established, I'm financially solvent and I have a slightly better wardrobe. But as good as things are, I am plagued by the feeling that whatever currency I now hold would have an exponentially higher market value if I were just ten years younger. A thirty-seven-year-old with a genuinely fulfilling and reasonably lucrative career, a decent marriage/non-catastrophic divorce under her belt, an overpriced-but-worth-it apartment and multiple intersecting circles of friends new and old? Fantastic! The future is incandescent. The present is a sweet spot engineered for maximum forward momentum. A forty-seven-year-old with all of this? Whatevs.

I'm sure when I'm fifty-seven I'll look back on logic like that and want to smack my forty-seven-year-old self for being such an ingrate. But for the time being, the cognitive dissonance can sometimes take my breath away. I teach in the same graduate program that I myself attended more than twenty years ago. A few of my colleagues, now probably in their sixties, were professors back when I was a student. There's something wonderful about this, something that confers a sense of both achievement and coziness. Less wonderful is coming to terms with the fact that when I was a student, I saw these professors as old. If you'd asked me their ages, I would have thought about it for a minute (having never specifically thought about it before) and pegged some of them for being in their sixties (which was definitely old to me at the time). I now realize they were the age I am now.

Does this mean that my students think I'm in my sixties? The notion seems preposterous, though given how the twentysomething mind works, it also makes perfect, if devastating, sense. When you are, say, twenty-five, the adult world is a simple binary construct divided between the young and the old. Young is anyone under forty. Old is anyone over sixty. There is no in-between. The forties and fifties don't exist. The forties and fifties are just a couple of lost decades in which the only goal is to try to maintain whatever operation (child rearing, career building) you got started in your twenties and thirties. And because this maintenance is so easily overlooked, so unsexy, so perennially under the radar, it is entirely possible for a twenty-five-year-old graduate student to look at her forty-seven-year-old instructor and unconsciously assume her to be a senior citizen.

This is a horrifying contemplation. Yet it's just one of a cluster of thoughts that make up the current of constant low-grade shock I feel about how old I've managed to become. At forty-seven, I could easily be a twenty-five-year-old's mother, the irony there being that if such were the case, I might actually seem even younger because I'd be up on pop culture and other youthful things that in my present state I don't know or care about. Most of the time, I'm relieved not to have to know or care about these things. My only exposure to contemporary popular music are the play-lists inflicted on me in group fitness classes, and I can't help but think that being forced to listen to them is the sonic equivalent of being put in tortuous positions in order to tone my butt. If endless squats at a ballet barre can maintain some illusion of youth in the body, maybe blasting Kylie Minogue can do the same for the mind. I'm using Kylie Minogue as a hypothetical because the truth is I have no idea what songs are being played in my barre class. And I'm pretty sure that given the choice between listening to Kylie Minogue and listen-ing to a Vitamix blender, I'd choose the blender.

I'm not proud of feeling that way. In fact, it terrifies me. Given the correlation between aging and death, declaring that you can't stand today's music might actually mark the first stage of the dying process.

And that brings me back to my apartment window, looking down at the river while listening to the same music I listened to in 1997. The big picture for me these days might be a mélange of sadness and puzzlement and oddly exhilarating resignation, but in this fleeting moment, it feels nearly perfect. I have work that feeds my brain at the same time that it pays for that supermarket sushi. I have nearly a half-century's worth of friends, which is something that is mathematically impossible to have in your twenties. These friends are in practically every time zone on the globe, and even when I haven't seen them in years, I can count on them to lift me up or crack me up or at the very least impart some kind of gossip that makes me think about human nature in a whole new way. I'm paying more rent than I can afford, but somehow I'm affording it anyway. The surface of my desk is as littered with paper napkins and hair accessories as it was twenty years ago, but I've met my deadlines anyway. Except for the ones I've missed.

My 1997 self would be satisfied with how things turned out, at least until I told her this was us at forty-seven and not thirty-seven.

'Is this as far as we got?' she might ask. 'Ask me in ten years,' I might answer.

Except I already know the answer. It's as far as we got. It's as far as we were ever supposed to get. I may not always live in this apartment or even in this city. I may not always live by myself. I may grow tired of the sushi. But on some cellular level, it will always be Friday evening, 8 p.m., alone at a messy desk. No matter what I do, my situational pendulum will swing back to this place. As anticlimactic as that is, it's also just as it should be. Everything has its set point. Except the rent, of course. The rent always goes up.

– Basically Dead –

January 2019

I think a lot about being dead. Not necessarily dying (I try not to think about that) or death – but deadness, specifically my own eventual state thereof. I think about lying underground and decaying into the earth, my flesh feasted upon by parasites and spores, my bones eroding into the soil, my organs liquefying and being siphoned up through tree roots. As though listening to a yoga instructor tell me to relax each body part, one by one, during the final savasana portion of a class – release your left foot, exhale out your right shoulder, let your spleen melt into the floorboards – I imagine the incremental corrosion of my carcass. I imagine the passing of a season or two until wildflowers grow over me like a blanket.

I run through this sequence of thoughts at various times of the day and night; when I'm lying in bed trying to fall asleep, when I'm sitting at my desk trying to work, when I'm stuck in traffic staring at a mile of tail-lights stretched out ahead of me on the highway. You might find this morbid; to me it's soothing. I'm still in my forties, reasonably happy and, as far as I know, perfectly healthy. But there's something almost meditative about conjuring my physical being in a state of active disintegration.

I don't know how or when I'm going to die, but I do know that when it does happen, I want a green burial. (Loved ones, please take note.) Sometimes called a 'natural burial' (though definitions and standards of 'greenness' vary), this is when a body is buried, without embalming, inside a shroud or container that can decompose right into the soil. The gold standard of green burials takes place on land trusts that have been set aside as permanent conservation easements and are maintained according to certain restoration ecology principles, but these, unsurprisingly, are few and far between. The next best thing is often a hybrid cemetery, which offers burial areas that minimize environmental impact by using only biodegradable caskets and shrouds and never burying embalmed bodies.

Many religions, such as Judaism and Islam, practice natural burial anyway, so in that sense, it's not particularly exotic. It should also be said that cremation rates have increased steadily over the last several decades and now account for just over half of body disposals. But considering that the funeral industry still puts more than a million-and-a-half tons of concrete and more than four million gallons of formaldehyde-soaked embalming fluid into the ground every year – and that a traditional cremation spews out carbon dioxide and even mercury into the atmosphere – the rest of us would do well to consider natural burial for carbon footprint-reducing reasons, if not religious reasons. (For what it's worth, there's also an ecological cremation method called promession, which uses liquid nitrogen to turn cremains into biodegradable freeze-dried powder.)

Admittedly, it was a cable drama that got me thinking about green burial, specifically the third to last episode of the last season of *Six Feet Under*, in 2005. After five seasons of watching the Fisher family, proprietors of a multi-generational funeral home, embalm bodies and peddle expensive caskets, we see prodigal son Nate buried in a cloth shroud and covered with dirt in an unmarked grave, in accordance with his wishes.

My interest in green burial has intensified in recent months, in part because of the death of my father. We'd never talked about how he wanted his remains handled, so his ashes now sit, in a box, on a shelf in my apartment, awaiting some final resting place that remains to be determined. When my mother died nine years ago, we fulfilled her wishes and sprinkled her ashes in a public space which, I now realize, was illegal. In both cases, the process felt – and continues to feel – chaotic and insufficient.

Since I have no children, the chaos of my own death could very well become the burden of someone I'm not even related to. I want to keep that burden as minimal as possible. I already cringe when the utility guy comes every month and has to read the electric meter in the back of my mortifyingly messy closet in my mortifyingly messy bedroom. The idea of loved ones rifling through my stuff looking for instructions on what to do with me postmortem is too distressing to contemplate. But the more I think about it, my recent interest in the subject has nothing to do with physical extinction – my parents' or anyone else's. It's more like cultural extinction.

'We're basically dead,' a fellow forty-something said a few months ago during a conversation about how we feel geriatric despite technically being in early middle age. 'Nothing we grew up with or cared about when we were young even exists anymore, so we sort of don't exist either.'

I have some version of this conversation at least weekly now. Sometimes it's about how young people don't want our advice anymore because nothing about our past experience – 'Pass out your business card at networking events!' 'Look for potential romantic partners in bookstores!' – is relevant to the world as it is now. Sometimes it's about the fact that no matter how digitally adept we are, we'll never be 'digital natives' and therefore will never be able to compete in the job market with people who effectively have college degrees in social media influencing (what we used to call 'communications'). Almost always, the conversation ends with us shaking our heads and wondering aloud if all this griping is just a generic byproduct of aging; if rather than talking about the revolutionary cultural shifts, we're merely barking out our version of 'get off my lawn'.

Is this why I want to literally sink into a lawn? Is it why I devoted an inordinate amount of time last week to researching the Infinity Burial Suit? Also known as the 'mushroom death suit', this is a garment lined with hybrid mushrooms meant to break down corpses while also removing them of toxins and sending nutrients back into the earth. Its creators are also the founders of the Decompiculture Society, an organization devoted to promoting 'intimacy with and acceptance of the physical realities of decomposition as vehicles toward death acceptance.' Now operating as a company called Coeio, it sells the mushroom suit for $1,500 as well as a range of other burial products, including mushroom-infused pet burial shrouds starting at $75.

The mushroom suit, which looks like footie pajamas as might be worn by Obi Wan Kenobi, doesn't appeal to me as much as the idea of just being wrapped in a piece of linen and left to my own devices. The nagging question is where I can be buried and whether I should try to get in on some real estate now. I'll probably never reside in the kind of place that would allow me to be buried in my own backyard, appealing as it may sound (though perhaps less so for anyone who might want to sell said land after I'm gone). There's also the frustrating fact that California, where I often live and suspect I'll die, doesn't offer any conservation trusts and the handful of hybrid cemeteries are in places I don't feel a personal connection to. That includes Woodlawn Cemetery in Santa Monica, which can be a real schlep in traffic from my stomping grounds on Los Angeles' east side.

At some point during my research, it dawned on me that a great place to be buried might be the Nebraska prairie, where I lived for several years in the early 2000s and to which I feel a strong spiritual connection. By strong spiritual connection, I'm referring to multiple attempts to buy some kind of dilapidated farmstead on which I pictured myself strolling through the tall grass in a cotton dress and possibly even a sunbonnet. These attempts were all thwarted either by recalcitrant sellers or my own chickening out, but the allure remains.

For a moment, it all seemed so right. I'd go directly into the heartland soil in nothing but a cotton dress, where I'd decompose and eventually be reincarnated as a Willa Cather paperback. But then it occurred to me that my body would have to be transported to Nebraska, and that would be a hassle for those involved; worse, even, than the commute from the east side of LA to Santa Monica. Maybe better to stay in California after all. But then I checked the prices at Woodlawn Cemetery: $17,617.50 for an adult green burial space, not including required funeral services! There's the west side for you.

'We're basically dead.' The sentence imprinted

itself in my brain the moment I heard it and I can still feel it there pressing upon me.

Recently, while buying an overpriced coffee, I triumphantly presented the barista with exact change, after digging around furiously in my wallet.

'We don't accept cash,' he told me.

My immediate thought was that somehow the coffee was free. But obviously, that wasn't what he meant. What he meant was that they accepted only debit or credit cards or some way of paying on your iPhone that I would never consider. What was also obvious was that I was basically dead. 'But, but,' I thought to myself, 'I just dug up $4.68 in exact change! That includes a nickel and three pennies, rare coins!' The cashier, who I'm certain had a man bun in spirit, if not in actuality, looked at me with actual pity.

I think about going back to that coffee shop wearing a mushroom suit and demanding that I be allowed to pay in legal tender. I imagine the barista looking perplexed as I explain, 'You're staring death straight in the face right now. This is what it looks like! I'm decomposing right before you!'

Ancient Greeks buried their dead with coins in their mouths so they could pay the ferryman to cross the river Styx to the underworld. Maybe my generation will resume this practice, burying each other with cash that's no longer needed in the era of Venmo and Apple Pay. And maybe my generation, by virtue of our precocious obsolescence – and increasing life spans – will also have so much time to think about our deaths that we start making some space for burial plots that don't cost upwards of $17,000.

For now, though, I'm wondering if my visceral need to decay into the loamy earth speaks to some sort of visceral need to be relevant, to feel a tactile connection to people, places and things. Maybe the idea of being eaten by microbes and fungus has something in common with the feeling of handing someone your business card, talking to a stranger in a bookstore, strolling through prairie grass in a cotton dress or simply paying with cash. Maybe this obsession with being dead is actually fantasy about staying alive in ways that seem no longer possible, or at least no longer useful in today's world.

Recently, a screen grab went viral that showed a news graphic outlining birth years for generations that are currently alive; the silent generation, baby boomers, millennials and post-millennials. There was only one problem. Generation X, a small but very real cohort tucked between the baby boomers and the millennials, had been left out. On social media, many Gen Xers responded with our characteristic appreciation for the irony of it all, even a wry satisfaction.

'Exactly as it should be! Wouldn't want it any other way!' The solidarity was moving, even inspiring. I had to wonder if 'basically dead' is, in some perverse way, a form of better living.

– Species Of Grief –

May 2019

A few days after the long-planned memorial service for my father, I put my dog down. My father had died six months earlier after a relatively brief illness. My grief over him had been a slow, steady trickle, a constant if generally manageable sadness. It was different for Phoebe, my Saint Bernard: a relentless firehose of anguish. For days, I did little but sob. Any activity I associated with Phoebe – and this included walking, sitting, eating and sleeping – was now so punctured by her loss as to be almost intolerable. Though my apartment had been heavy with my father's effects for months – tax files, photographs, his forwarded mail – Phoebe's accoutrements threatened to turn the place into a museum of melancholy.

For days, her water bowl remained on the kitchen floor, still filled, as if she might come back at any moment. Reaching into coat pockets, I'd invariably pull out one of the ubiquitous plastic bags I carried around to pick up after her outside. Opening my backpack one morning, I happened upon her leash and collar, which I'd stuffed inside after the vet handed them back post-euthanasia, and then crumbled to the floor. When my housekeeper, Emelie, arrived for her monthly cleaning, I contemplated paying her in full and sending her away because I couldn't bear the thought of permanently ridding the apartment of dog hair. Emelie, who'd loved Phoebe (as had her kids, who she often FaceTimed while cleaning my place), grew teary at the news. I, in turn, was too choked up to speak. All I could do was flail my hands around and apologize for being such a mess.

'Don't take this the wrong way,' a friend said later, 'but you seem more upset over your dog than your dad.'

I did not take this the wrong way. I took this as a perverse article of faith. Losing a parent is terrible. Losing a pet is shattering. Both occurrences are more or less inevitable. We all walk around this earth knowing our parents will eventually die, if they haven't already. (The alternative, dying before they do, always falls into the category of catastrophe.) Similarly, to have a pet is to know that it will almost certainly die before we do. The pre-scheduled heartbreak is just part of the deal.

So why did losing Phoebe feel so much worse than losing my father? Maybe because my relationship with her was built on loss to begin with. She came into my life six years before, shortly after the death of my last dog, a creature I'd loved more fiercely than anything before or since. I was married at the time, and though my husband and I hadn't planned on getting another dog right away the house was so unbearably quiet without a pet that we'd signed up to be dog foster parents.

Phoebe, a stocky, tanklike animal whose snub-nosed, mushy face and red-rimmed eyes gave her the air of a sad, out-of-shape prizefighter, had recently been rescued from backyard-breeding methamphetamine dealers in the California desert. When she was found, Phoebe was still nursing ten puppies, all of which were eventually adopted after being showcased on a local television news broadcast. (Indeed, they were so gigantically adorable that they'd been scooped up by staffers at the news station.) Their mother looked young enough to be a puppy herself.

The arrangement was supposed to be temporary, but within hours of her arrival, Phoebe made it clear she'd be staying. She lay under my desk all day while I worked, allowing me to rest my toes on her hindquarters like a slobbering, snorting footstool. She used the dog door like a pro, refrained from chewing on the furniture and never stole food, even if it was at eye level – which our dinners nearly always were, given our habit of eating off the coffee table while watching one of the cable dramas we used as a substitute for emotional intimacy.

Phoebe turned into a strikingly beautiful dog: 120 pounds with a thick and gleaming (if endlessly shedding) white-and-brown coat and soulful brown eyes that always suggested a human consciousness lurking inside. Her health and disposition, on the other hand, presented challenges. Within a year, Phoebe was diagnosed with arthritis and spondylosis, conditions common to giant breeds that were irresponsibly bred. She had hyperthyroidism, then hypothyroidism, then hyperthyroidism again. It was also posited that she had mild brain damage due to early exposure to methamphetamine. Though Phoebe spent most of her time dozing and loudly snoring, her waking life featured moments of such extreme excitability that she routinely knocked over furniture. She became so giddy at the prospect of going for a walk or a car ride that she had twice hurled herself into the front gate with a force that would have given another dog – and certainly a human – a concussion.

In addition to her astonishing physical strength, Phoebe was a champion drooler. When she leaned her head against the window near the back seat of the car, slobber dripped down the glass and into the door, where it finally caused an electrical short and rendered the window inoperable. During walks, Phoebe had a habit of lying down and refusing to get up. She often pulled this maneuver in busy intersections, which left us frantically trying to stop traffic while she rolled around on the pavement.

'I'm looking at this dog,' a vet said to me once, 'and seeing a Prozac type of dog.'

When I said I didn't feel right giving my dog psychotropic pharmaceuticals, the vet sold me a plastic collar for $75 that was supposed to secrete soothing pheromones for a month, at which time it would need to be replaced by another $75 collar. Within hours,

Phoebe had wiggled out of it. She was a creature who simply refused to be soothed. Except, arguably, by me. She followed me when I walked out of a room. She barked inconsolably when I shut her outside. Often it seemed as though all she really wanted to do was lie under my desk.

Eventually, my marriage broke up. Needing to put space between my husband and myself, I loaded Phoebe into my ancient Volvo and drove across the country with her to New York City. The idea was to stay for a year or so, but nearly four years later, for reasons I'm still trying to figure out, she and I were still there, keeping each other company amid the lingering sting of divorce. With her head-turning looks and limited athleticism, Phoebe turned out to be the perfect urban dog. Though she lunged at pit bulls from the end of her leash, she calmed down considerably once we settled in the city, like a restless suburban teenager whose angst was alleviated by the sheer act of becoming a New Yorker. Phoebe generally thrived on a few short walks per day, but she also loved to take long strolls through the park and even went with me to the second Women's March in 2018, where young girls in pussy hats fawned over her and posed with her for selfies.

That march turned out to be one of her last major outings. In the ensuing months, Phoebe resumed her habit of lying down spontaneously during walks in the middle of city streets while I frantically directed traffic around her. She began slipping when walking up stairs and lying down in the elevator, even as the doors threatened to close on her.

A veterinary neurologist diagnosed Phoebe with wobbler syndrome, a disease of the cervical spine that would eventually render her unable to walk. Miraculously, for nearly a year, steroids kept her mostly upright. She couldn't walk farther than a block or so, but she loved nothing more than to hang out on the park benches across the street from our building, which we did for hours in all but the coldest weather.

The day my father died, I sat with Phoebe on the benches and watched the late-afternoon autumn sunlight break off into strips of indigo and violet. My father had died unexpectedly in his apartment early that morning, going into cardiac arrest even though doctors had been hoping to treat his early-stage cancer with surgery. That summer, before my father knew he was ill – or at least before he'd admitted it to himself – I brought Phoebe to my father's girlfriend's house in Staten Island, and we all sat in the yard drinking gin and tonics and eating salami and crackers. One perk of Phoebe's encroaching infirmity was that she'd stopped lunging at other dogs – she couldn't get on her feet fast enough to bother – and on this occasion she happily socialized with a corgi and a border collie.

'Eventually she won't be able to walk, and I'll have to put her down,' I remember saying.

My father asked how long I thought that might

be. I said maybe six months. I didn't really mean it. It was the kind of prediction you make to keep it from coming true. Besides, my real concern during that visit was my father. He appeared almost shockingly thin and a little jaundiced. At one point, he lost his balance and tripped on a rug. I asked what was going on.

'Well, I'm slowly dying,' he said in a way that sounded like he didn't really mean it.

Three weeks later, my father called me to ask, his speech alarmingly slurred, if I could meet him in the emergency room at New York Presbyterian Hospital. I was eight hours away, teaching at a writing conference in central Virginia. I'd brought Phoebe with me in the Volvo, since her mobility was too quirky to entrust to a dog sitter. I immediately packed us both up (including the collection of yoga mats I'd brought so Phoebe wouldn't slip on the hard floors of the pet-friendly hotel room) and raced through the night back to New York.

My father died eleven weeks later. Phoebe died six months after that. My father's death makes me feel like the ceiling of the world has been lowered. I've learned to get by in that constricted space, constantly ducking my head to avoid hitting that ceiling. But Phoebe's death is a different proposition somehow. Phoebe's death makes me feel like someone has come along with a giant eraser and rubbed out my face. When you live in New York City with a Saint Bernard, people see the dog first and you second, if they see you at all. Phoebe was my face. To many of my neighbors, who knew her name but not mine, she was my entire personality. She was the main thing about me.

The dog that came before Phoebe, a mystery mutt named Rex, who was also large and astonishingly beautiful, was with me for thirteen years. That means I haven't been dogless for nearly two decades. In that time, I have gone from being a young woman to a not-so-young woman. I have gone from being someone who could attract attention without a dog to being someone who attracted attention mostly because of her dog. When Phoebe and I were together, everyone who passed us acknowledged us in some way. On the rare occasions when I was solo, I blended into the sidewalk, just another pedestrian. Now that I'm solo all the time, I go mostly unnoticed, or so it feels. And because my current situation does not allow for a dog (I have a book coming out later this year, and months of travel obligations to go with it) I am going to have to figure out how to live this way for a while. I am going to have to learn to exist without a face. And possibly without a personality.

That facelessness should be an interesting look, if hardly a unique one. It's the look of growing older, which I'm beginning to understand is in no small part the look of loss. Maybe the key is this: Don't take it the wrong way. Take it as inevitable. Or as an article of perverse faith. We're all slowly dying. It's just that pets and parents – the ones who see us even when we're invisible to ourselves – tend to leave us first. It's the natural order of things – that is, if we're lucky. And sometimes even the best luck, it seems, is still perfectly devastating.

– Playlist Of Tears –

February 2020

I 'm not sure when it started, but at some point over
the last several years I replaced listening to music
with listening to people talking. Looking back, it must
have happened slowly, in increments. First, I began
passing over the usual rotation of songs in my iTunes
library in favor of some addictive podcast like *Serial*
or *S-Town*. Instead of Tom Waits or Aimee Mann
accompanying me on my daily errands, I'd find myself
on the edge of my subway seat listening to a true crime
podcast in which a murder (along with the social,
economic and psychiatric conditions surrounding it)
was endlessly parsed and potentially never solved.

Later, the political climate turned following the
news into something like a round-the-clock assignment. So I dutifully stuffed my brain with news analysis – everything from *The Daily* to the *Slate Political
Gabfest* to good, old-fashioned NPR (yes, on the actual
radio) – in the hope of hearing something that would
help me make sense of the world. That effort being the
fool's errand that it obviously is, I'd load up on even
more podcasts, many of them analyzing the analysis
itself. Whereas once I might have listened to a classi-
cal music station while eating dinner, I now listened

to disembodied voices – not even talking heads but talking ghosts – having conversations about obscure issues I only knew about thanks to other conversations I'd listened to while eating breakfast. (I live alone, as you may have gathered.)

I should clarify that music isn't gone entirely. I'll have my iTunes on shuffle when I go out for a run, stopping frequently to type in my phone password in order to scroll to the next song, which tells you something about my seriousness as a runner. Whenever I rent a car out of town, I listen to music almost exclusively, partly because the novelty of Bluetooth technology and being able to access my phone from a car dashboard (my own car is twenty -years-old and has a cassette player) still has me in awe. A few times a year I'll find myself at some kind of live music event: jazz in the park or one of the chamber music salons my neighbor hosts periodically. For the most part, however, music – at least the foreground kind, the kind you choose based on your mood, the kind that makes you feel like a kid listening in your room even if you're old enough to have a whole house – has largely left my life.

I can't blame this on the cacophony of politics and the whiplash of the Trump presidency, since this all started well before the 2016 election. Nor do I think it has that much to do with the emergence of podcasts. There may be more than one million podcasts out there, only a small fraction of which anyone actually listens to, but they're still dwarfed by the number of music recordings available – mostly through streaming services. On Spotify, which I rarely use (I like to insist it's because it's 'bad for artists', but really it's because I find it overwhelming) 20,000 new tracks are added each day. Individual music downloads have been on the decline for the last several years (although vinyl began making a niche comeback in 2006 and actually outsold CDs last year).

There are 43 million songs available to purchase on iTunes and, according to at least one estimate, the average iTunes user has a library containing 7,160 tracks. My own Apple music library has thousands of songs covering hundreds of artists and albums. In my ancient Bluetoothless car, cracked CD cases and shamefully scratched discs and battered cassettes cover the backseat the way dog hair still covers the interior walls and ceiling – despite the dog no longer being around.

So it's not like there was a day over the past few years when the music died. What's happened is that as I've grown older there's scarcely a song in my iTunes library that doesn't make me so sad as to render it almost unlistenable.

That statement is so dark I almost didn't write it, but there it is. And when I try to figure out how I got to this place, all I can think is that it's not just music we're talking about here but the soundtrack to a life. And that is a very different thing than just a bunch of songs.

My music collection may exist in the form of

digital files now, but it was once made of vinyl records played on turntables in my childhood bedroom, cassettes in my Sony Walkman in high school and college and discs loaded into the CD player of my towering 'stereo' in dingy, early adulthood apartments. As such, it mapped itself across the plains of my life trajectory. This is what music does, of course. It embeds itself into our emotions, often burrowing far deeper than the memories of the events that spurred those emotions. From there, the songs we love become the half-life of our emotions. They are whatever's left of whatever was going on at the time.

I may not remember every detail of the summer of 1987 (it was a big one, since it was the first summer I could drive on my own) but the music I listened to during those months – Suzanne Vega's second album, *Solitude Standing*; the XTC album *Skylarking* – will forever be knitted into the thrilling, slightly chaotic sensation of pressing a gas pedal and moving myself forward. The early months of college may be a blur, but I cannot hear even four seconds of a track off Kate Bush's *The Kick Inside* (though the album was a decade old by then) without smelling the Pine-Sol and cigarette smoke of the dormitory halls.

In the last few years, though, my music collection became a minefield in which any given song, if allowed to play past the first few seconds, has the potential to blow a crater of sorrow right below my feet. A search for music has me clicking past tracks as if they were disturbing photos from which I have to avert my eyes. *Not that one;* it's what I was listening to in the early divorce days. *Not that one;* it's from the dying mom year. *Not that one*; it's what was in the car CD player during that terrible summer after I turned forty.

Strangely, even music from happier, long-ago times has taken on a hue of melancholy. Not this one; it's what I listened to on the stereo in that first dingy apartment, back when my options were limitless if only I'd been able to see them. Even Pine-Sol and cigarette-infused Kate Bush, with all her college-era associations of higher knowledge and new love and the heady revelation that there are a million different ways you can be in the world, can send my mood crashing down so hard it breaks the whole day. Not just because there are no longer a million different ways I can be in the world but because I now realize there never were. There was only one way, the one that led me to where I am now – not a bad place by any means, but still one in which I cannot listen to most music.

Whereas I once organized my life around music, I now organize it around podcasts. In a way, I've come to avoid my own music as if avoiding pain. That's another statement so dark I almost hesitated to write it, but something tells me I'm not the only one in this pre-dicament. As someone noted to me recently: 'Music is alive with associations. I can't listen to some of it if it's too connected to a painful situation. Podcasts don't seem to hold those same associations for me.'

This observation was a response to a highly scientific poll I conducted on Twitter recently, asking my followers what they listened to more frequently, music or podcasts. If the answer was podcasts, I asked, 'was it because there's almost something too emotionally intense about music? Because music leaves you alone with your thoughts the way podcasts don't?'

The answers were split pretty evenly between music and podcasts, with many people adding audiobooks to the list of distractions (somehow I've never taken to these; preferring to hold books in my hands so I know how many pages are left). But a number of people offered thoughts similar to my own. One man said he preferred podcasts because 'music seems to largely dump unvarnished and unwelcome emotion into my frontal lobe these days.'

Another said this: 'A lot of my favorite music from teenage-young adult years has too many memories attached to it ("intense" is the perfect word to describe it because it's not necessarily good or bad). And at almost forty I find it impossible to discover or enjoy new music.'

Data does reliably show that most people's musical tastes are locked in by their early twenties, with the songs that are popular in our early teens occupying a special place, no matter how cheesy or terrible (I guess that explains my ongoing affinity for The Go-Gos, though they're not in my iTunes library.) That makes this phenomenon of age-related music avoidance all the more depressing. If the losses that pile up as we get older actually drive us away from the music that buoyed us in our youth, what's left? Are we destined to live out our days listening to the grating-if-charming vocal fry of millennial podcasters or the hyper-enunciated lullaby of audio books? Will we never sing in the car again? Okay, make that will I ever sing in the car again?

Maybe the solution, at least my solution, is to get a new car, one with Bluetooth so I can listen to my old music in a new way. Or force myself to listen to – and enjoy, god dammit – some new music. Or stop being such a sad sack about everything. Or stop having sad sacks like Aimee Mann and Tom Waits in such heavy rotation.

Or, if all else fails, make a seventeen-part podcast delving into the psychology of listening to people talking rather than listening to people making music. I would totally listen to that. It would probably make me so sad I'd go back to music.

–The Unbearable Halfness of Being –

August 2022

I t's shocking to add this up, but it has now been more than six years that I have lived with one foot out the door. By that I meant that I've been in a limbo state wherein I can't bring myself to make any long-term commitments, particularly with regard to where I'm living. This has caused me (allowed me?) to keep many things at arm's length. The list of concerns I've shoved aside because right now is only temporary range from seriously reckoning with my financial future to making myself available for any relationship, platonic or otherwise, that would require me to put anything on my calendar more than a month out. Meanwhile, that calendar flies by. The clock ticks. The future descends into the present. And yet I can't bring myself to step inside or outside of the door and just close it behind me already.

I mentioned this half-life sort of life on my podcast recently and, to my surprise, several people wrote to tell me they felt the same way. A few friends I know in real life also shared this sentiment, and that surprised me, because by all outside appearances they have both feet resolutely inside the door of whatever structure they've built for themselves: marriage, family, steady job, place of residence that they've actually occupied for more than a few years.

I'm batting zero on each of these scores. And even though this isn't exactly new terrain for me (I wrote an entire book about not being able to decide where to live), the past year has been a particular doozy. If I spent roughly the past six years with one foot out the door, the past ten months have been tantamount to lying across the threshold in a supine position, my fists clenched over my eyes as pieces of crumbling Sheetrock rain down on my face.

In January of 2022, I left New York City, where I'd been living since the fall of 2015, and returned to Los Angeles, the city where I'd spent the better part of the past two decades and which I'd never meant to leave for more than a year or two at the most. Trying to explain what took me so long to come back usually makes me embarrassed and then depressed, so I try to avoid the subject. Suffice it to say that it wasn't a relationship or a job or any normal, understandable thing like that. It was a series of situations that, for one reason or another, had me stuck in place.

At first it was because I was writing a book that engulfed my life for three years and had me forestalling any life decisions or plans until it was done. Three months after the book was published, the pandemic hit. Like everyone else during the pandemic, I started a podcast and got a puppy. The one cliché I avoided was starting a Substack newsletter, but that was only because the ordeal of finishing the book had burnt me out to the point where even writing the show notes to my podcast was excruciating. So I effectively stopped writing. The dip in my income soon followed. Which, let's face it, would probably have happened even if I'd kept writing.

Nothing about this situation in and of itself precipitates having one foot out the door of your life. But in retrospect, I can see that I was caught inside a trap of my own half-assed making. If I'd been totally miserable and totally broke, that would have been one thing. Instead, I was semi-miserable and semi-broke. My New York apartment had a spectacular view that I could have stared at around the clock (and often did stare at for several hours at a time). But it was a glorified studio with a Murphy bed, which I dutifully stowed away every morning. Pulling it down every evening, I died a little inside. How long are you going to keep living like this?

I asked myself this question as I walked to the subway in the knife-ishly cold winters and weepingly humid summers. I asked it while standing in Disneyland-caliber lines at Trader Joe's, where employees barked out crowd-control directives and carried signs on eight-foot poles reading 'End of Line' as if propping up disembodied heads on pikes. I asked it when I walked the dog around the block for the fourth time that day, berating myself for not walking him five or six times (or having a damn yard). I asked it as I circled the blocks of my neighborhood in my car looking for a parking spot.

I almost didn't include that last sentence because it's such a cliché. Every New Yorker puzzles over their life choices while driving around looking for a parking space. It's no different than going camping and remarking at how many stars there are in the sky. But I can tell you this: when I pulled out of town on a foggy morning in January and headed over the George Washington Bridge for all points west, it was like driving over a map of five years of empty promises to myself. By then, my ambivalence had become a source of embarrassment. I'd spent so many years telling friends I'd be returning to Los Angeles soon that they'd long stopped believing it. I imagined dying and being buried under a headstone that read SHE ALWAYS SAID SHE'D BE BACK.

The way I finally did get myself back to LA was to play the same mind game I'd played when I left. I wouldn't make any definitive statements or big commitments but would instead just get there and go with my emotional flow. Just as I had put my furniture in storage in LA in anticipation of my return, I would not give up my apartment in New York or move any of my things out but would do a little decluttering and rent it to subletters. I would take each day as it came. I would not throw a welcome-back party for myself but would instead slowly ease myself back into social activities. I would see how I felt.

In the beginning I found that I wasn't quite sure how I felt, so I decided to keep a calendar where I rated every day on a scale of one to ten and jotted down a few notes charting my mood.

Tellingly, there was never a day that rated less than a seven. Eventually, it was consistent nines and the occasional ten. The thing I like least about LA is that it can get apocalyptically warm even in the fall and winter, especially in the Eastside neighborhoods that comprise my main stomping grounds. One day in February the temperature hit ninety degrees and the air had that nervous, ghostly feeling you get when the days are short but the heat lingers well past dusk and the whole world seems poised to engulf itself in flames by morning. As I went about my tasks I was sure I'd be looking at a low score on my feelings calendar. But around twilight I emerged from a supermarket and was overcome with a sense of such peace and rightness that I nearly gasped. The air was suddenly cooler; the magic-hour light was like a cocktail that had taken the edge off the whole day. I rated the day a ten and stopped keeping the calendar after that.

Still, I made no commitments. I didn't register my car in California or get a new driver's license. I didn't change the billing address on my credit cards. There was little point in that anyway, since I lived in other people's spaces and had no real address, subletting a costume designer's exquisitely decorated house in a hilly Eastside enclave for five months and, after that, a documentary filmmaker's irremediably dusty Spanish colonial in the San Gabriel foothills for another three. For eight months, I lived among strangers' books and artwork. I used their sheets and towels and dishes. I took in their mail. I chatted with their neighbors. Every time I drove past the storage facility where my own books and artwork and dishes lay in wait, I died a little death. How long are you going to let your things sit in there? I could scarcely remember what I even had – a desk, some bookshelves, some rugs in God-knows-what condition – but sometimes I could almost hear my possessions crying out to me, mewling like a cat trapped in a garage.

How could you let this happen to us? How could you let this happen to yourself?

In July I went back to New York for a visit. My subtenants were in Europe and were happy to let me stay in the apartment if I deducted the days from their rent. For three days I sat at my desk and looked at the view. On the weekend, I drove upstate with a friend and looked around the countryside to see if perhaps that was a place I might want to live. For all my indecisiveness, I knew two things for certain. First, housing costs in Los Angeles were prohibitively expensive. Second, I could never again live in a New York City apartment with a dog, at least not with my particular dog, or at least not until he was geriatric and no longer interested in walking more than ten feet at a time.

But there was a potential third option. Perhaps I

could buy a place in upstate New York. This was in the realm of affordability; call it affordable-adjacent. Maybe I could even keep subletting my apartment and visit it occasionally, especially if I could hold onto my improbably flexible subtenants. Or maybe I could Airbnb the upstate house and live in the apartment. So many possibilities and combinations! So many doors through which to step halfway!

Still, as I tooled around the Catskills, all I could think was that the aperture of the region was too small. The tree canopies were too low, the hills too gentle, the sunsets kind of meh. 'I just can't get excited about this,' I said to my friend as we ate vegan stir fry in the requisite shabby-quaint luncheonette in an unhip-yet-somehow-full-of-hipsters town. 'I realize it's a character defect, but I can never bring myself to like upstate New York the way you're supposed to.'

'That's not a character defect' he said. 'Liking Los Angeles is a character defect.'

What can I say? I love how the hulking topography of the west enlarges the world's font size. I like the big mountains and the big ocean and the wide freeways and normal-size Trader Joe's. Flying back home at the end of my trip, I gazed out the window as the midwestern plains gave way to the southwestern desert and then the sprawl of LA exurbia. By the time we'd descended to a couple thousand feet above the ground and were floating past the downtown skyscrapers on the way to LAX, it was obvious to me that I was never going to shake my perverse, even inexplicable love for southern California. By the time I stuck my credit card into the pay station at the longterm parking at the airport and saw that it had cost me $500 to leave my car for less than a week, it was also obvious that I simply could not afford to live in either LA or New York City, at least not right now.

Upon this recognition ensued a month of mental real-estate chaos that's mortifying even by my standards.

The short version is this: having spent enough time in Zillow's rental listings to see that anything I could remotely afford would essentially amount to a converted garage with granite countertops and a sleeping alcove, I accepted that I would have to move someplace I could afford but where I didn't know a soul. From there, I decided that since my own misery was the only possible outcome, I was going to do what was best for the dog. Like a martyrish (codependent, borderline narcissist?) parent, I would sacrifice all of my happiness for his well-being and move to a place where he could romp around freely while I played Wordle and felt sorry for myself. As grim as it was to contemplate, I told myself this relocation would (naturally) be only temporary. I would suck it up, buckle down and let my cold-weather dog bound about in low-cost-of-living bliss while I worked non-stop in order to change my financial picture and go live where I wanted.

I went onto craigslist and typed 'large fenced-in

yard' in the sublet section of every city and state in America where the weather wasn't oppressively hot. This led to several correspondences with scam artists purporting to own rental property in Flagstaff, Arizona; Burlington, Vermont; and even, inevitably, upstate New York. While keeping an eye on private listservs and specialized sites geared to academics on sabbatical, I took to Googling random search terms that probably offer as good a glimpse into my psychology as you're likely to find.

Sublet large yard fenced pet-friendly Flexible lease dog okay hardwood floors Sublet farm fence dog central air

Then one day, while checking for updates on one of the referral-only listservs, I spotted it: an art-filled, tastefully designed converted barn in rural, mid-coast Maine on twelve acres, two of them fenced-in for dogs. I messaged the owner and she wrote back right away. She and her husband were artists with a soft spot for big dogs. They spent winters in a warmer climate and loved renting their house to other creative people, especially ones with big dogs. We exchanged several messages and she checked with the costume designer I'd be subletting from, who said I was a perfect tenant. The situation was perfect, perfect, perfect other than a few minor inconveniences.

The inconveniences included the following: after driving across the country from New York eight months earlier, I'd now have to turn around and drive all the way to Maine. Once I got there, I'd be a seven-hour drive from New York City, so this wasn't exactly the same as having a house in the Catskills. Further, I would be living in rural Maine for the entire winter, which would be great from a watch-the-dog-romp-in-the-snow point of view, but might have a few downsides in every other department. Finally, the sublet wouldn't start until November 1, and I had to be out of the dusty Spanish colonial on August 31.

The barn house owner was so keen on renting to me that she actually called around trying to find a temporary place for me to stay in September and October. When that didn't work, I took to Airbnb, searching in both mid-coast Maine and LA, since technically there was no reason I had to leave LA in September (other than that autumn is the most miserably hot season in LA and, now that I was prioritizing the dog, it would be better to skip town by then).

Finding next to nothing, I was about to give up and rent a semi-dilapidated 'rustic cottage' in Tujunga on a month-to-month basis when I found an Airbnb in Maine that would take a dog and at least had a partially fenced yard. With all the extra fees and taxes, it added up to a small fortune, but it was in the town nearest to the barn house and I figured it would be good to mix with the locals for a while before holing up in the country. I pictured myself going to a cozy tavern and meeting a sexy, weather-beaten fisherman who would then be on call to help me when the power went out or if I saw a mouse. Oddly, I also pictured myself going to AA meetings just for something to do.

I began preparing to move to Maine, which is to say I made an appointment to have my car serviced and mentally braced myself to drive exactly 3,158 miles, which somehow conjured the image of being sucked into a black hole. I decided a way to mitigate this would be to take my time and see friends along the way, so I reserved some stays in Denver and in Lincoln, Nebraska, further racking up my Airbnb tab. For the better part of two weeks, I was in a near-manic state, deciding that I should also host a series of podcast-related events along the route, maybe even record live shows from bars or bookstores or wherever such events are held. This led to worrying about having the right audio equipment for such a thing, and one night I lay awake for hours fretting about how this would all go and, additionally, whether I could leave my dog alone in the Airbnb during said events. Not that he wasn't fine being left alone, but the question was, would I be fine? The thoughts piled up from there. I could bring the dog to the events, but then he might act up and I'd be distracted. Of course, if I'd trained him better he wouldn't act up at all. In Maine I would work harder on training him. But what if I was too cold? What if I perished in a car crash on the cross-country trip and never got there at all?

What happened next is the thing that always happens next. I took one last look at the Zillow rentals in LA and saw something I could almost afford. I texted the property manager and, unlike 99 percent of property managers, he texted right back and said I could come look at the place in an hour. It was a small, unfancy but charming house in the shadow of the San Gabriel Mountains, on a street lined with both pine trees and palm trees. It was a regular lease, not a sublet with someone else's furniture. Given the number of applicants competing for rentals, I figured I'd never get the place, but nonetheless the first thing I did after seeing it was run back to my laptop in the dusty Spanish colonial and cancel the Airbnb reservation in Maine, which was hours away from exceeding the two-week cancellation period. Then I wrote up a lease application in which I explained that I really, really, *really* wanted the house and that I would be the best possible tenant, even though I lived with the canine equivalent of a musk ox and did not have a regular paycheck.

Before I tell you what happened after that, I'll tell you this. Last spring, a friend who's deeply into astrology did my chart. In the middle of telling me all the good things that were on the horizon (my finances would improve; I would take ownership of my emotional needs; I might have room for romance in my life but not until January, when Mars moves into my first house), she paused and said nothing for a few seconds.

'Oh no. What is it? What are you seeing?' I asked, even though I don't believe in astrology at all.

'You are . . . unsettled,' she said. 'Your sense of home. It's all over the place.'

At the time, this was a relatively new friend. She did not know the details of my housing history, which made it suddenly obvious to me that astrology was real.

'Pluto is in your fourth house,' she said. 'Your constant need to change is a compulsion.'

'Sounds about right,' I said.

'There is nothing worse than never feeling settled in the fourth house,' she said. 'It would be torture for many people. But you manage it because you have to. You even put it to creative use. But the unsettledness is a constant in your life.'

'Will it ever end?' I asked.

'It will change,' she said. 'It won't end.'

To my shock, I was offered the small house among the pines and palms. My first reaction was relief that I didn't have to drive to Maine. I wrote several large checks to close the deal, which was exciting but also made me embarrassed all over again about changing my plans. The barn house owner was gracious about the whole thing, but it turned out I'd missed the Airbnb cancellation deadline by an hour and ended up losing $3,000, which is a pill so bitter I can taste it in my mouth long past swallowing it. (Yes, I fought it. I fought it from every possible angle for more than a month. But retired couples in Maine drive a hard bargain.) On a more positive note, I moved my things out of storage. When I rolled down the storage unit door for the last time, I figured I surely had both feet on the other side of it.

Except that as I write this, I'm sitting at my desk in my apartment in New York, waiting for the midday sun to shift to the west so I can open the drapes again and see my computer screen, as well as my view. My subtenants are away again and I am here for a week. I know this arrangement is only furthering my chaos and uprootedness, but the fact is that despite the Murphy bed and the one-roomness of it all, I irrationally love my apartment. I love it the way you love someone with whom you're in a dead-end relationship that you none-theless can't bear the thought of losing.

At least, that's what I tell myself. But the other morning, when I walked in after getting off a red-eye to JFK, I thought: this love isn't irrational at all. This love makes perfect sense. How can you not love a beautiful apartment in New York City? And how can you not love the hours just before dusk in Southern California? How could you choose one side of the door over the other when you have two perfectly good feet?

This is the end of this essay. It's not the end of this story, but insofar as I've written the story right up to the line of its unfolding, it's as far as I can go now. Another casualty of living with one foot out the door is that, if you're a writer, it's nearly impossible to get the kind of perspective on your life that's required for putting something interesting about it on the page. One of the biggest lessons I impart to my students is not to write about your experiences until those experiences are sufficiently in the past. Otherwise it's like trying to paint a self-portrait while you're smashed up against your own mirror. This essay is a violation of that lesson. But it's also a long overdue step back into my life as a writer. And since that life has always taken place on both sides of the door, maybe this is just the way things are meant to be. Maybe Pluto moved into my fourth house because that house is on many acres of land and fenced for dogs. In the meantime, I'm living in a small house in California. Don't ask me where my feet are.

– 70 Million Songs –

October 2022

Recently while settling into my seat on a flight from Philadelphia to Los Angeles, the pre-recorded boarding announcements informed passengers that in addition to selecting from hundreds of streaming options on the in-flight entertainment app, we could access Apple Music in order to 'enjoy more than 70 million songs.'

70 million. This made for an especially strange contemplation because it so happens that about a month ago I downloaded a new album (don't ask me what album; it doesn't matter) and have been listening to it non-stop on repeat ever since. (Does anyone use the word 'album' anymore? It sounds outdated, but 'record' makes even less sense.) There's one song I like so much that several times while driving I've played it four or five times in a row, hitting the backtrack button on the steering wheel again and again like a dope-addicted rat hitting a lever.

It's crossed my mind that this musical sugar coma might be a mental health warning sign, for instance a presentation of low-grade OCD or the kind of depressive episode that robs you of the will to advance to the next song. But the truth was that I'd been congratulating myself for listening to anything new at all. Most of the music in my iTunes has been there for twenty years or more. Discovering a new artist had me thinking maybe my tastes weren't as sclerotic as I'd feared.

But being able to choose from 70 million songs reminded me all over again that my engagement with contemporary culture is near zero. 90 percent of music, movies, television/cable/streaming series (is there an umbrella term for this genre we used to call 'shows?') I've never heard of and will never see.

There is something almost surreal about this, given that once upon a time I might have been described as someone who 'inhaled culture'. In my twenties, as the internet was just beginning to peek out over the horizon, I had a pretty solid grasp on the 'arts scene', as we called it back then. I couldn't have told you what was on exhibit in every Soho gallery, but I knew what films were in theaters and how long they were staying there, what important novels had just come out, what shows were worth watching on television (not much back then), what venues my favorite musicians were playing, what big exhibits were at the big museums and even what was being performed on Broadway or at the Metropolitan Opera – not that I ever went.

Back then, I went to the movies at least twice a week, often alone, as was my preference. I'd take the subway down to Film Forum or the Angelika and read the *Village Voice* cover to cover, paying particular attention to the arts criticism. One of the great pleasures of my filmgoing was re-reading the reviews after having seen the movie. It was like hearing a recording go from mono to stereo. Suddenly you understood the big picture. You knew what everyone was talking about.

Somewhere in the mid to late aughts, it stopped being possible to know what everyone was talking about.

For at least the last decade I haven't known what anyone is talking about and for the last several years I haven't really cared. I do not say this with pride. It came up on one of my podcasts the other day – the one I do with my thirty-year-old co-host – that I'm unfamiliar with the story of *The Little Mermaid*. For my co-host, that story is as timeless as *The Night Before Christmas*. Not knowing that Ariel lives in Atlantica (I've since Googled this) is like not knowing that Santa Claus lives in the North Pole. But I was already a sophomore in college when the original Disney film came out in 1989. I was sitting on dorm room floors with my classmates using flashcards to study for our Intro to Art History survey class. The course material started with the Greeks and went all the way up to the present. It was overwhelming, like drinking out of the proverbial firehose. It also, of course, stopped in 1989, since that was as far as the present went. Nearly every evening I went to a screening of whatever movie the college film league was showing that night (on 16-millimeter projectors that were forever slipping out of focus or breaking down).

I remember having a conversation with a classmate about whether it was possible to take in too much culture. After a certain point does consuming art drain you of your ability to make it? If so, what is that point? How do you know when you've reached it?

More than thirty years later, I can't say exactly when that point occurred, but I know it happened a while ago. Well before I was hearing announcements about a 70 million in-flight song selection I was starting to feel so overwhelmed by what we now call 'content' that the only way I could cope was to ignore 90 percent of it.

That means I only consume the exact specific things I want to consume. My brain is lopsided. I know nearly everything there is to know about the current gender identity movement, including everything J. K. Rowling has and hasn't said about it, but I haven't read a single Harry Potter book. I honestly didn't know that Joe and Jill Biden had a daughter named Ashley, or any daughter at all, until a friend mentioned it over brunch a few weeks ago. This came up in the context of a news story about her diary being stolen and then exposed by right wing video makers.

'Who?' I asked. 'Ashley Madison?'

'No, Ashley Biden,' my friend said. 'You seriously don't know who she is?'

My friend had made pancakes with fresh blueberries from the farmers market in Hollywood. I was sitting with him and his husband at their kitchen table,

64

gazing out a huge window onto a tangle of jasmine, hibiscus, palm trees, bamboo and bougainvillea: classic Los Angeles breakfast scenery. It wasn't yet 11 a.m. but outside it was already hot and unnervingly humid. It was one of those days where you feel like California is cheating you out of itself. I drove home listening to my new album on repeat. Did Joe and Jill Biden have any other kids I didn't know about? I wondered if I should embark on a strict diet of new information. Perhaps every morning, before the algorithm spirits me away to my preferred subject areas, I should force myself to explore a topic I have no interest in whatsoever.

The day I boarded the plane with 70 million songs had a dystopian feel from the start. At the airport in Hartford, where I'd begun my trip, the TSA agent removed two large, unopened tubs of expensive cream cheese from my bag and held them over the trash. (Let's put aside for the moment why I was carrying this amount of cream cheese.)

'You can't bring this onboard,' she said.

'But it's not a liquid,' I said.

That I was bothering to have any conversation at all about this was a mortification.

'It's considered the same as a liquid,' the agent said.

The agent then started to say something about taking my things and going back to the security point entrance. I assumed she was going to finish the sentence with 'and check your bag.' Instead she said 'and eat it.'

'You think I should go back and eat two containers of cream cheese?'

'It's an option,' she said.

For a moment, I actually considered it. Not because it was really an option but because there was something obscene about allowing her to effectively throw fourteen dollars in the trash. Also because it would be after midnight when I landed and if I checked my bag I'd be waiting at the carousel for forty-five minutes for the sake of cream cheese.

'Can't you give it to someone?' I asked. 'Do you want it?'

In the end, the cream cheese went in the garbage. But you already knew that. The TSA agent rolled her eyes and looked at me as if she was embarrassed on my behalf. You probably knew that, too.

In the Philadelphia airport, before getting my connecting flight to LA, I tried to order a roasted vegetable salad at a concession stand on the concourse. The cashier explained that in order to do this I had to download an app onto my phone, enter my email address and place my order, which would be instantly transmitted to another screen in the kitchen. Through a glass partition, I could see the cooks, masked and gloved. One was looking at me impatiently, as if waiting for me to decide what I wanted. The cashier, for his part, was not behind the counter but stationed in front of it for the very purpose of helping people use the app.

'Can't I just tell you my order?' I asked, like a two-hundred-year-old.

'No, but I can walk you through it,' he said.

'What is the point of this?' I asked.

He explained that it was a Covid measure, a touchless order and delivery system designed to limit close physical contact. When I couldn't get the app to open after several tries he finally just took my phone and placed the order himself. I paced around for six minutes until it was ready, then made a dash for my gate. During the flight I ate the salad, listened to my album, did some work on my laptop, listened to the album again.

The next day I came down with Covid. I spent the better part of the next eight days on the couch, watching a British comedy I thought was brand new even though it was actually fifteen years old. A friend brought groceries and left them outside the front door. Inside the bag was soup, bananas, a package of bagels and a container of cream cheese.

– Independent Creator –

March 2023

One of my earliest childhood memories is of my father excoriating me over a gift someone had given me. I can't pinpoint exactly how old I was, but I couldn't have been more than six, since the incident took place in the small rental house my family occupied in Austin, Texas, in the mid-1970s.

This is what had transpired: a girl lived across the street who was my frequent playmate. She was three years older, and because of this I worshiped every square inch of ground on which she stood. Also because of this, I'm sure she didn't appreciate my company nearly as much as I appreciated hers, but she was generally patient and generous with me, lending me her knotted yarn bracelets and so on. One day, after a few hours of playtime at my house, she told me she had to leave because her mother was taking her shopping at the mall.

'Can you bring me something?' I asked.

By which I mean I apparently asked. I have no recollection of the actual moment, only a piercing and indelible knowledge that the moment occurred. I do remember the neighbor girl returning to my house some hours later and presenting with me a small coloring book; the kind of thing that was probably eight pages long and cost twenty-five cents. I think it might have had an Easter theme, since I recall a yellow cover with a bunny or egg illustration. In my memory, my mother wasn't home and my father was in enough of a supervisory role to notice that I had something new in my possession and ask where I'd gotten it.

Maybe I said something like, 'She went to the mall and I asked her to bring me something.' Or maybe the other girl, with her three years of seniority, managed to convey something more precise. In any case, my father entered a state that seemed to skip right over anger and go straight to something like panic.

The way I've always pictured it, we were all standing in the bathroom and my father had backed me up against the wall while my playmate stood haplessly in the doorway. I'm not implying anything violent when I say 'backed against the wall'. But my memory has always staged this scene in such a way that my father was physically blocking my escape until I said some combination of magic words. It might be assumed that those words were 'I'm sorry', but I honestly don't think my father wanted me to apologize as much as he wanted to put the whole incident into his Teac reel-to-reel tape player (possibly his most prized possession) and rewind it into pre-existence.

I'm pretty sure I was crying hysterically at this point, not least of all because my revered neighbor was witnessing the whole hideous event. It's possible I ended up giving the coloring book back to my neighbor, at my father's behest. It's possible that she returned the next day and, clearly under orders from her own mother, gave me the coloring book all over again. It's also possible that none of this happened and is instead some oddly assembled mental casserole thrown together from random anamnestic ingredients. But given my parents' authoritarianism when it came to asking anyone for favors, material goods, or help of any kind (that is, asking anyone but them), I'm 90 percent confident that this memory is at least 60 percent accurate.

My father had grown up extremely poor, raised by a single mother who was too proud to take welfare. This was always the explanation for the maniacal aversion to asking for help. My mother, for her part, had a nearly equal aversion to displaying any kind of need – economic, emotional or otherwise – and tended to enforce my father's strictures. Every Halloween, a struggle session ensued over trick-or-treating. My father likened it to door-to-door begging. My mother thought it was a tacky practice for any child older than eight.

As with many disputes with my parents, I fought back until I was not only exhausted but forced to admit that I agreed with them. I mean, how could you not? It's obvious that Halloween is a low-rent holiday. It's clear that asking friends – or heaven forbid, their parents – for rides home from school is presumptuous and puts them in an awkward position. Don't get me started on having an unrequited crush and admitting as much to anyone, least of all the object of the crush. This is a no no no no NO of such magnitude that even writing this sentence makes me wince because it suggests that I have, in fact, wanted things from people that they were not willing or able to give me.

So I spent the next several decades asking for as little as possible. Given my penchant for moving to new homes more frequently than some people change their car oil, that's really saying something. A highlight reel of my early-to-mid adulthood would show a dozen scenes of me single-handedly dragging around heavy pieces of furniture because I'd rather drop a futon frame down six flights of a tenement stairwell than risk being characterized as 'needy' by whatever upper-body-strength-havers I was hanging out with at the time.

Meanwhile, my parents, to their credit, never betrayed their principles. When my father had his first heart attack, he walked to the hospital rather than bothering anybody for a ride. When my mother, who in her later years lived alone in a small apartment, became terminally ill and I had to spend months helping with her care (not that she asked for that help directly), her across-the-hall neighbor lent me an extra bedroom so I wouldn't have to sleep on the couch. In her morphine-induced delirium, my mother was confused by this arrangement, then alarmed. 'Are we paying her?' she asked.

When I got married, my mother's most resolute piece of advice was this: 'Don't even think of having a gift registry. It's tacky.'

Which leads me to the barbaric state in which I now find myself. After decades of earning a living as a writer and being paid by corporate media entities – and, even better, relying on agents to negotiate that pay – I'm now in the economy of independent creators. That means instead of receiving checks that have passed unceremoniously through multiple layers of faceless payroll channels, I get my money directly from readers and listeners.

It's a good thing my parents aren't alive to witness all of this; if they were, it would kill them. I'm fairly confident they would have preferred to have seen me working at a big-box store rather than hustling on Substack. If my mother had been forced to choose between worrying that her friends would spot me stocking shelves at Walmart and worrying that her friends would receive an email inviting them to pay $7 a month for my 'content', I guarantee she would have chosen the former. And not just because she wouldn't have believed any of her friends shopped at Walmart.

The thing is, I understand this perfectly. Because truth be told, there's a little part of me that craves a job at Walmart (okay, maybe Costco). Amid the relentless churn of content creation and site management and emails from people yelling at me because the podcast won't play on an Android app or some item of merch (yes, I sell merch!) is sold out in XL or boy, was your last episode a disappointment, I sometimes entertain elaborate fantasies about working a grunt job. I imagine waiting tables at some sad diner in some ragged, forgotten town off the interstate. I imagine punching a clock at a Goodyear tire factory. I imagine packing Prime orders in an Amazon warehouse like Frances McDormand's character in *Nomadland*.

Those scenarios fall firmly into the category of fantasies you know you'd never want to realize. (Though the Goodyear factory isn't totally random; twenty years ago when I was broke and living down the road from a Goodyear plant outside Lincoln, Nebraska, I thought seriously about filling out an application.) But as stupidly naive as they are, I sometimes wonder if they're really that much stupider or more naive than the notion of someone like me – who was forbidden to sell Girl Scout Cookies because it 'puts too much pressure on people' – trying to monetize her entire life through crowdfunding.

When you think about it, the new creative economy is more or less a digital, non-stop version of trick-or-treating. Every day, every hour, creators are thinking of new ways to get attention and knocking on doors in hopes that they'll get it. In turn, the subscribers throw out small increments of money like cheap candy. As on Halloween, these ventures can be charming at the start of the evening, when the solicitors are little and cute and convey an endearing innocence about the whole racket. But when it's 10 p.m. and packs of teenagers who've barely cobbled together costumes are banging on the door demanding mini-size Snickers that they'll swallow in one bite, it all becomes rather tedious.

Am I telling my Substack readers to cancel their subscriptions? God, no, since the money that sputters through here is as close as I have to a regular paycheck. But if they sometimes ask themselves why they're handing over their hard-earned cash to all these creators, know that we creators are asking ourselves that same question. That is to say, we're also asking why people are handing over their money. At least this creator is. And though the answer still often eludes me, my response is always the same: thank you a million times over.

As for my parents, if they're looking down on this carnage from the afterlife, all I can say is 'please forgive me'. I know not what I've done, or even really what I'm doing. I only know that as poorly cut out for this job as I am, I'm probably even less qualified to work at Walmart. Still, a girl can dream.

– What I Have In Common With Trans Activists –

March 2023

Y ou'll notice (if you are given to noticing such things) that there is nothing in this book about the new gender movement. This is by design, as any exploration of that subject is all but guaranteed to hog the spotlight and I'd hate to do that to the other innocent essays in this otherwise-unsullied-by-this-issue collection. It would be like having a bunch of kids and putting one of them on a reality TV show while ignoring the others. That said, the massive spike in young people identifying as something other than their biological sex fascinates me and I've devoted countless podcast episodes to the question of why this is happening. As such, I'm often asked why I'm so captivated. The short answer is, How can anyone not be? In the pantheon of grand psychosocial displacement events, I can't think of a richer and more labyrinthine tapestry than this one. The longer explanation is too long to go into here, but by way of isolating one particular segment of that explanation, I'll say this: when I see the way many gender-dysphoric young people can get manically focused on transitioning, often to the exclusion of just about everything else, there's a piece of me that understands on a visceral level where they're coming from.

That is to say, I get how personal pain can lead to a life of obsessive confirmation bias. When it comes to being in a frame of mind in which nothing but the obsessed-upon subject is allowed entry into the brain; when it comes to spending nearly every waking moment searching the internet for stories that echo your own story (and shielding your eyes from those that don't); when it comes to making a full-time job of showing everyone around you how great your life is because, unlike them, you know how to live authentically and not like some conventional normie Basic – guess what? I get it. That's because there was once a time in my life when I was so filled with angst about an aspect of my identity that I literally couldn't think about anything else.

It was the time when I was coming to terms with the fact that I'd never wanted kids and wasn't going to change my mind.

I was in my early forties and recently married. Yes, this is a relatively advanced age at which to be a newlywed, much less be grappling with the question of eleventh-hour parenthood, but being a holdout on anything related to domesticity (except the actual buying of a house, which I was determined to do before thirty-five) had always been a point of pride. Although my husband and I had started off equally ambivalent about having kids, the early years of our marriage had pushed us toward a certain clarity. Unfortunately, it was in opposite directions. My husband realized he wanted to be a parent. I realized I did not.

Because our marriage was at stake – and because there were subtler, more pernicious problems that were not nearly as easy to articulate as this one – I set about trying to talk myself into wanting to be a mother. This involved a lot of mind games wherein I told myself I'd send the kid for long stints at summer camp before starting boarding school at age ten. When eventually I was forced to admit that on the deepest, most cellular level, I'd never wanted to be a mother and never would, I entered a new phase. In today's parlance, you might call it 'cope'. I set about trying to talk everyone into believing that not having kids was not only a morally superior way of being but an extremely common way of being. In fact, not wanting kids might be just as common (if not more so!) as wanting kids. We just didn't realize as much, because societal judgment kept most people from being their true selves. Though not for long – a revolution was coming.

Sound familiar? These are the kinds of things you hear from trans activists, especially the ones who insist that the massive spike in trans identification among young people is a naturally occurring phenomenon. There's no social contagion, they say. Trans people have existed since the beginning of human civilization; they just haven't been able to come out until now because of oppressive patriarchal norms that reinforced the myth of a gender binary. Meanwhile, young people experiencing gender dysphoria (the real kind or the aspirational kind) fall down Reddit and Tumblr holes so deep there's no trace of light left when they look up. Invigorated by their persecution complexes, they are nonetheless 'exhausted' by everything in the world that does not reflect their own image back to them. Pretty soon, they're not living in the real world but in a walled city of their own confirmation bias.

I lived in this city for several years in my early forties. It was a lonely place, which is saying something since I spent a lot of time insisting that it was a bustling metropolis, brimming with vivacious, fully evolved people who'd cracked the code to a happy life by not having kids. Never mind that most of these people lived on subreddits with names like r/childfree. Never mind that I fed my confirmation bias by typing things like 'I regret having kids' into Google and reading post after heartbreaking post from anonymous parents whose abusive partners and/or high-needs children had handed them life sentences of hard, thankless labor compounded by guilt, shame and constant financial strain.

Because I focused on these stories and blocked out all the normal happy stories (including those told by my own friends who enjoyed being parents and were living perfectly fulfilled – if temporarily sleep-deprived – lives), I became certain that any given parent had at least a 50 percent chance of ending up with a child whose debilitating mental or physical health issues would effectively imprison that parent for life. From there, I extrapolated that anyone who was single and searching for a partner with whom to start a family was engaged in a socially engineered scavenger hunt fueled by mass delusion. In a display of myopia that astonishes me to this day, I even took part in a public 'debate' with some researchers from the National Marriage Project in which (as best as I can recall) I argued that early marriage was bad for society because people change and grow over time, and isn't it better if a mature tree meets another mature tree and they grow old together in the forest than if two young trees get together too soon and grow into a tangled mess?

I definitely lost the debate, though at the time I was pretty sure it was at least a tie. Afterward, one of my opponents came up and said, 'You made some interesting points, but you seem to be forgetting that most people want to have children, so they can't wait so long to get married.'

He was right. I'd forgotten that entirely.

Here's the part where you start to suspect that the lady doth protest too much. It would follow, after all, that the reason for my defensiveness and selective hearing was that deep down I actually longed to have kids, but feared it was too late. Anyone observing my behavior during those years might have understandably concluded that I was grieving the loss of potential motherhood and, consciously or not, channeling my pain into an almost perverse denial of reality.

They would have been half-right. I was grieving, but it wasn't over not being a mother. It was over losing my marriage. Although my husband and I were dear friends and in accord on many fronts, it had become increasingly clear that our marriage didn't have the legs to go the distance. Moreover, if he truly wanted kids and I truly didn't, we would need to cut our losses sooner rather than later. For this, I felt inconsolably guilty. That guilt, layered on top of the slow drip of impending divorce, had turned me into a deranged evangelist for a non-existent (or at least pretty niche) cause. In my obsession, I even embarked on a book project wherein I commissioned essays from writers who'd chosen not to have kids. (Sometimes obsession has its upsides.)

I'm not suggesting that this experience lines up neatly with the fanaticism we see in aspects of the gender movement. These are two very different kinds of issues. And make no mistake, I'm certainly not saying that gender dysphoria itself isn't real. What I am saying is that I know what it is to be in pain and to try to quell that pain by convincing yourself that half-truths – or even non-truths – are facts. In my case, the half-to-non-truth was that the 'joy of parenthood' was a sham and people who bought into it were suckers who were secretly envious of my life.

Moreover, because I felt so alone in my pain, I was

determined to construct a world in which there were not only lots of other people like me but vastly more people than is commonly recognized. Like gender activists who insist that the only reason we didn't see more trans people in the past is that the world wasn't safe for them, I desperately wanted to believe that the only reason most people had kids was because society forced them into it. That might be a little tiny bit true, but of course it's mostly not true. The majority of people, women and men alike, want to be parents. People like me, who genuinely don't feel the urge to procreate, may have been slightly overlooked historically, but we are still outliers. And guess when I was able to admit that? As soon as my marriage was over and the whole question of having children was removed from my life's equation. I might have still been in pain from the divorce, but the ceasefire on this particular issue provided instant relief. Before I knew it, the entire subject had dropped off my emotional radar.

Since then, I've devoted very little thought to my status as a never-parent. Unless I'm being interviewed on a podcast about my book (which, funnily enough, was a *New York Times* bestseller on the 'child care and parenting' list), it rarely comes up. I have no urge to make a case for there being lots of people like me out there, and in fact have registered some concern about the U.S. population falling below the replacement rate (though I'm not quite sure how concerned to be about that).

As it turns out, I like being an outlier. Even better, I like forgetting that I'm an outlier. When someone asks if I have kids, I'm almost always taken by surprise, as if they're asking if I have parakeets or a timeshare in Aruba. If I were still in distress over this issue, I might experience that question as a microaggression. I might feel 'othered', even if I'd never use that word. But now it's just another moment of chitchat. My life isn't a movement or a revolution; it's just my life.

Oh, the banality of it all! I feel lucky to have gotten to this place. I also feel obliged to recognize that so many of the mental contortions and attempts to reroute reality that we see in trans activism are not expressions of genuine ideological commitment as much as emanations from a bottomless well of emotional pain. When you're terrified of acknowledging yourself as an outlier, you'll do anything to create a new norm, including pointing to an obvious fiction and insisting that it's a fact.

Take it from the person who spent years trying to make a case against human reproduction as a default biological imperative. Or actually, maybe don't. The way things are going, I may turn out to be right about that.

– Problematized –

May 2023

S omeone I know from the literary world recently
    emailed me to ask if I'd be her interlocutor when
she came to my city on her upcoming book tour. I was
elated. I used to do this sort of thing all the time but
haven't been asked in years.

In fairness, no one gets asked to do anything anymore; at least it can feel that way. Live events were
decimated by the pandemic and are unlikely to make
a complete comeback. But in my case, something else
might be in play as well. When it comes to literary
events, I might be a tiny bit canceled.

Or maybe not. Honestly, I don't know. But falling
out of favor with your old crowd is kind of like being
exposed to a virus. Whether or not you're actually sick,
you still risk spreading your contaminant to others,
so there's a moral obligation to tell people what they
might be getting into by being in your presence. That's
why, as excited as I was by the prospect of sitting in
the event space of an indie bookstore with a handheld
mic and asking a fellow author 'about your writing
process', I felt the need to make sure my friend was
comfortable putting me on the bill.

So I explained that while everything would almost

surely be just fine – besides, this was her event, not mine – there was possibly a certain kind of (purely hypothetical) indie bookstore employee that maybe kinda sorta would be less than jazzed about my participation. I added that since she and I had last crossed paths, there was also possibly a certain kind of book buyer who might wince at the sight of my name on an events calendar. I suggested that she might want to contact the bookstore events manager and float my name alongside a few others and gauge the response. (The fact that authors are now charged with coordinating their own events is a whole other pitiful matter.)

I also suggested that I was probably crazy for thinking all this and she should take it for what it was worth. Also, I had no idea what it was worth.

Of course I'm crazy. Writers are crazy. I'm also not blind.

Ever since the publication of my last book, which made an honest appraisal of the culture war, I've been somewhat non grata in certain literary circles. There's nothing too special about this, since it's a pattern that has played out for all kinds of people in all kinds of milieus since the Trump election. The exact opinions and observations that had made me the toast of the town in 2015 were getting me removed from guest lists little more than a year later.

When my book came out in 2019, publications that had once heralded me were running reviews with lines like: 'There are so many potential angles of attack on this deeply silly book that it is hard to know which to choose.' Sometimes the reviewers were people I knew socially. On my own book tour, more than one purportedly friendly interlocutor seemed to turn on me as soon as the show started, framing questions as sly accusations, as if afraid the audience would see them as being on the wrong side.

Or maybe I was just paranoid. That's the worst part of this whole mean-girl, gaslight-y racket. You're never quite sure if you're just imagining things.

It's possible you stopped getting invited to the party because you didn't toe its ever-narrowing line. But it's also possible – in fact, it's undeniably true – that there aren't nearly as many parties as there used to be. Or maybe you fell out of favor not because of anything you wrote or said but because you're older than you once were and the party organizers favor the young. Or maybe you should just publish another book already. After all, it's been a few years. With all that extra time on your hands, you'd think you could have written a couple hundred continuous pages and slapped them between two covers. (As long as it wasn't about the culture wars, which is the only thing you're interested in, and maybe you should examine that.)

This is the thought sequence running on a constant loop through my mind. It's torturous in its solipsism, but it's also pretty typical of people who, like me, once traveled freely through the universe of ideas but have in recent years been encumbered with baggage we'd never imagined carrying. That the suitcases are mostly empty – what's in this baggage is all reputational, a feeling people have about us – is immaterial.

I'm not talking about being canceled. I am not canceled and never have been. A few times, people have implied otherwise to me: 'What is it like to be canceled?' I've been asked: how do you handle it? Are you upset? But this is absurd. I am not the least bit canceled. I walk the earth. I go to restaurants and have friends and get zillions of emails from people asking for favors and advice. In what I can't help but regard as the definitive barometer of writerly viability, I still get asked to review books for the *New York Times*. How canceled can you be in that case?

I haven't been canceled. I've been problematized.

That's my word for it, anyway. I'm not a pariah, just problematic. I'm canceled-adjacent at most.

What does it mean to be problematized? It means instead of people getting in your face and calling you a fascist or a TERF or a Karen, they just talk behind your back. Complaints against you are mostly confined to the back channels. As a rule, you don't present useful opportunities for virtue signaling, since you're neither famous nor legitimately controversial. So instead of dragging you on Twitter, they cluck about you in Slack channels. They add you to Reddit lists of baddies to watch out for. They don't get you fired; they just keep you from getting hired.

Something I've noticed about cancel culture over

the past year or so is that it's acquired something of a cool factor. As much as no one wants to be actually canceled, there's a certain street cred in saying you were. I've heard people say, 'I got so canceled over that!' and then go on to describe a single incident wherein a few friends or colleagues got angry about something they did and gave them the cold shoulder for a few days.

Public figures are routinely referred to as having been 'repeatedly canceled', an oxymoron that calls to mind the countless deaths of Wile E. Coyote in the old Warner Bros. Road Runner Show cartoon. In each episode, he'd be blown up in a dynamite explosion, flattened by a train, crushed by a boulder, or otherwise hoisted on his own roadrunner-obsessed petard. Yet he was always right back moments later, unscathed and ready to continue upholding the classic parable of quantum insanity: doing the same thing over and over and expecting different results.

Does that make Wile E. Coyote the ultimate 'cancel-proof?' Or does it just show how little cancellation means anymore?

Legitimate cancellation can be devastating, especially when it involves ordinary citizens permanently losing their livelihoods over hysterical nonsense. (And to anyone who tells you they've never heard of people like that, I say: of course you haven't; those people have been canceled.) But the number of canceled wannabes running around makes me think that cancel culture has canceled itself to the point where it's just well . . . culture. Often when people say, 'I was canceled', what they're really saying is, 'I was noticed'. Frankly, I'd rather be problematized. At least that comes with a little mystery.

After a few emails back and forth, my author friend decided it would be fine for me to be her interlocutor. As long as you don't think it would keep people away, she said. I conjectured it might be the opposite; perhaps it would bring in a crowd. (No guarantees, obviously!) People are drawn to those who embody the complications they can't untangle in themselves. That's why we read novels. That's why we love hearing stories about the problems of others. Problems are inextricable from the human condition. So maybe being problematized is a form of being humanized.

I'm starting to think that being problematized is something to aspire to rather than avoid. Unless you lead a very boring life and never open your mouth to speak, you're going to be problematized sooner or later. It's a virus, after all. So you might as well stop living in fear. Just don't call yourself canceled. It's an insult to canceled people. And to yourself.

– A Handsome Woman –

Maybe it's because my chief adversary has always been my body, but I've never had a problem with my face. I've actually always liked my face. For most of my life, my operating assumption has been that my face is quirky but reliably cute, occasionally even pretty. The defining feature is my chin, which ranges from gently triangular to downright pointy, depending on where I am in the five-pound window of weight I tend to slide around in. From as early as I can remember, I was told I had a heart-shaped face and that this was a good thing. I was also told by my mother that while my body would always be a problem (given that her body was a problem, it would only follow that mine would be too, since in her mind we were the same person), my face was pretty and I was lucky not to have to worry about it.

And so for the better part of fifty years, I didn't worry about my face. In fact, I enjoyed it. Throughout my entire adolescence, I didn't have a trace of acne. Though my narrow jaw required multiple tooth extractions and several years of orthodontia, including an appliance that widened my upper palate, I even enjoyed having braces. Back then, braces were what signaled to the world that you were no longer a child but a bona fide teenager. And since I wanted nothing more than to grow up and be a mature person in the world, all that metal in my mouth felt like an on-ramp to freedom.

Although my extremely fine, extremely straight hair presented some frustrations, I mostly dealt with this by having a short haircut, which I felt I could pull off due to the high quality of my face. I never wore makeup and was well into my twenties before it even occurred to me that I should maybe put on some mascara and lipstick if I was going to a wedding or formal event. As far as I was concerned, my skin was flawless, my cheeks were rosy and my eye color contrasted nicely with my hair color, so what was the point of makeup? Besides, I had more important things to think about, for instance how much I hated my upper arms.

Decades later, the situation has somehow reversed itself, or at least shifted the contents of its neuroses. While I mostly tolerate my body, I suddenly hate my face. My chin, which invited comparisons to Reese Witherspoon's from almost the moment the actress first appeared on-screen, now strikes me as requiring its own zip code. My nose, which I never gave a second thought to, looks slightly wider than I'd ever perceived it to be. Though my skin is still decent and I seem thus far to have avoided the jowls and turkey neck that all of my contemporaries are obsessed with, the heart shape that was once so central to my identity appears to have hardened into something closer to a downward-pointing kite.

Sometimes when I look at myself, I think I look like Jay Leno in drag. Other times, I feel my wide nose and wider eyes make me resemble a Muppet. In some of my lowest moments of moral and physical self-appraisal, I am visited by the chilling notion that at some point when I wasn't paying attention, I went from being a pretty girl to being a 'handsome woman'. The horror this elicits makes me ashamed of my vanity, which in turn makes the horror that much worse.

When I say 'look at myself', I'm not talking about looking in the mirror. I'm talking mostly about looking at myself on the computer screen, often within the confines of a 16:19 ratio box with 1,080 pixels. This is not a flattering medium for anyone, but when you are an aging woman who looks like a Jay Leno Muppet, it's a hall of carnival mirrors.

I've been podcasting for the past three years and, last summer, since one podcast is not enough, I started another one with a woman who is more than twenty years my junior. She is brilliant, opinionated and unapologetic in her worldview, which is occasionally hilariously at odds with my own. She is also young and beautiful, which only became relevant early this year when we accepted that it is a truth universally acknowledged that you can't grow your audience unless you surrender to video and YouTube.

So now, every week, instead of sitting around in

our sweats or pajamas and recording three hours of conversation about the news of the day, we put on decent clothes, apply makeup, style our hair, declutter our 'studio' backdrops and fire up the expensive lights and cameras we were advised to purchase in order to look professional. Then we attempt to talk about current events and philosophical concepts without veering out of the frame or, in my case, rocking back and forth, which apparently is something I do while talking that, for more than half a century, I hadn't the faintest awareness of. The most memorable (ideally outrageous) moments of these conversations are then isolated and cut into promotional video clips in which our heads appear in silhouette cutouts alongside episode titles like 'Hateful Nerds Need Love, Too' and 'Babies, Breast Implants, and Disgust!'

From a vanity standpoint, it's hard for me to say which is worse: the promo clips, which tend to capture my face in a freeze frame of unflattering mouth contortions, or the videos at their full length, which, as far as I'm concerned, are about 20 percent me looking sort of okay and 80 percent my own personal re-enactment of *The Ring*, the classic (2002) Gore Verbinski paranormal psych thriller about a videotape that causes death to anyone who looks at it.

My podcast partner, for her part, has dewy skin and the kind of lustrous dark hair that cameras love. Unlike me, she doesn't need reading glasses to see the screen, so she's not constantly adjusting them and shifting her gaze around to try to avoid glare from those expensive lights. I try to avoid the YouTube comments lest I spot something that will bruise my ego even beyond the injuries I already inflict upon it. But when I do peek at them, they're full of viewers extolling my partner's youth and beauty. (Did I mention that she also hates the way she looks? Do I even need to mention it?)

I hate that I'm forced to wear my reading glasses on the YouTube podcast, but recently I discovered that there's something even worse: not wearing them. Tasked with recording a quick introduction that did not require reading anything off the computer screen, I removed my glasses, imagining the audience gasping in surprise: 'Why, Miss Jones, you're beautiful!'

When I watched it back, I was shocked. My eyes looked tired and even lopsided. My chin looked even more prominent than usual, and not just because I didn't have the benefit of eyeglasses to draw attention in the other direction. Out of nowhere, my chin seemed to be showing traces of marionette lines, giving me the vague appearance of a Chucky doll. This is not a podcast intro, I thought. This is a horror movie.

The truth is, my face has always been a complex proposition. I might have passed most of the time for 'conventionally attractive' (blond hair helps), but I've always been aware that the attractiveness is entirely dependent on the angle. I have one of those faces that can go from pretty to homely with just the slightest tilt of the head. Generally speaking, I look decent facing head-on, but the profiles get tricky. That's where my chin abandons its post at the bottom of that heart shape and becomes something more like a rock protrusion. 'A Habsburg chin,' someone called it on social media years ago, commenting on a photo accompanying some article I'd written. I didn't know what they meant until I made the mistake of looking it up and seeing they were referring to the 'mandibular prognathism' common to the dynastic Austrian family and thought to be a result of inbreeding.

For all I know, there could have been inbreeding somewhere in my not-too-distant heritage, as my father's paternity was effectively unknown, and no one in the family ever seemed interested in finding out more. My chin is my father's chin; there's nary a trace of my mother there. This is a dark thing to say out loud, but the reason I hated my body and not my face is because my mother saw herself in my body but not my face.

Though my upper arms were an heirloom passed down on her side – if you must pose for a picture in short sleeves, always bend your arms so they look slimmer, she told me when I was six – my chin was out of her jurisdiction, not her fault or responsibility. And since my father's self-loathing did not extend to his appearance, it never occurred to me to dislike my chin. In fact, I liked my chin precisely because it looked nothing like my mother's. Since everything about her appearance was (according to her) wrong, anything that wasn't like her was, by definition, right.

So even as I did constant battle with my body (the details are so typical as to be barely worth mentioning), I made peace with my face. When I was nine years old, a friend's parents went to see *Kramer vs Kramer* and subsequently decided that I looked like Meryl Streep. Looking at pictures of myself from the time, I can almost see what they meant. More importantly, even though I did not grow up to look like Meryl Streep, I decided at some point in my early twenties that I was cursed – or blessed – with what I deemed 'Meryl Streep Face Syndrome', which is what you have when you can look strikingly beautiful from one angle and then almost monstrously misshapen from another.

That's not to say I was ever strikingly beautiful or that Meryl Streep has ever been close to monstrous. But let's be honest; some faces are simple and some are complex. And simple faces can withstand a far greater range of conditions. Sometimes those conditions are called 'regular photo with no filter'. I once saw a series of tweets from a portrait photographer expressing exasperation and even sorrow at the way her subjects reacted to their own images. So accustomed were they to the trusted filters and reliable head tilts of their own selfies that seeing their actual faces reflected back at them – sometimes on actual film – was so shocking as to be devastating. People have no idea what they look like anymore, the photographer observed. Worse, they have no idea what people look like anymore. It's not unlike what you hear about the effects of pornography. We've become so inculcated by digitally enhanced images that our blueprint for sexual excitement is effectively a piece of AI. Faced with a flesh-and-blood human being, actual disgust can set in.

But whatever happened to that old adage about everything looking better in black and white? (In 'Kodachrome', Paul Simon sang that everything looked worse, but it was obvious that he meant the opposite.) Film cameras could be merciless in more ways than one, but when they were good to us, they were very good. As a young author, I posed for steely black-and-white portraits – on real film – many times. This was at least half the point of being an author. The sessions lasted for hours, and you had no idea what you looked like until such time as you saw that now-artifact known as a contact sheet. I'm pretty sure I hated the vast majority of shots on the vast majority of contact sheets, but the handful that made the cut are worth a thousand of even the best digital photographs in the eras that followed.

In 2005, in what is still one of the most awestruck moments of my life, the revered portrait photographer Marion Ettlinger, known for her photos of famous authors, called me and asked if she could take my picture simply because she liked my writing. The resulting photos, fall into the category of the photo itself being beautiful but the subject being kind of strange-looking. I love the photo even though I kind of hate how I look.

A fairly widely circulated photo of me, probably taken in 2000, appeared on the back of my first book, *My Misspent Youth*. Shot by the photographer and filmmaker Alix Lambert, it's a black-and-white image of my thirty-year-old self standing in front of a wall of graffiti in downtown Manhattan. It's a close-up, so you can't really see the graffiti, but it's there in spirit, which is to say it's there in a way that you can only capture with real film. Also, I'm pretty sure I'm wearing no makeup whatsoever.

Twenty-plus years and many lifetimes after the fact, a man I was dating stood in my apartment and pulled the book off my shelf. 'Whoa, I recognize this photo,' he said. 'At a bookstore in Boulder in 2001. I remember seeing it and thinking, "Now, that is some-one I'd like to know."'

'Did you buy the book?' I asked.

'Well, no,' he said.

That is someone I'd like to know. What more can you ask of a face than that? Sure, it's nice to be the object of desire, admiration, even envy. But the highest compliment that one human can pay to another is an interest in actually knowing them. In 2015 or so, after I did a literary event on a stage, a woman came up to me and asked if she could paint me sometime.

'The planes of your face are very unusual,' she said. 'It would be a challenge to paint you.'

I knew this was a form of flattery – sort of. I also knew that what she was saying was that I looked good from certain angles and dreadful from others and that this represented a kind of aesthetic puzzle. I recall her handing me a business card, which I've long since lost, but I think of her every time I saddle up for yet another YouTube recording. I have a Post-it above my desk on which I've written STAY STILL, CHIN DOWN in giant letters. The less head movement, the less often I'll veer into a bad angle. The more I can keep my chin down, the more I can avoid looking like a Habsburg with a YouTube channel. As for my glasses, they're never coming off again.

I haven't even mentioned Botox and dermal fillers. What can I say? I've both done them and not done them. If I could afford it, it's possible I'd do them more, but at the end of the day, I don't actually think they make much of a difference. I have a dermatologist in New York with whom I have a friendly enough relationship that she feels comfortable cheerfully berating me for not loading my face up with Juvederm.

'Look at this,' she'll say, pulling up one side of my face. Then she'll point to the other: 'And look at this. See the difference?'

'I guess so,' I'll say. But I honestly can't see the difference, partly because I don't have my glasses on.

How has it come to this? How, after building a career for thirty years, has my value been reduced to a thumbnail photo and the appraisal of barely-postadolescent YouTube commenters? I know, I know . . . that's just the sound of my distorted thinking. It's not really like that. No one is actually saying that my intrinsic value is only as high as the quality of my appearance on a video box. But somehow, we've arrived at a moment in which artists and thinkers of all ages are subject to appraisals not just of their ideas but of their physical selves, often poorly lit and awkwardly framed. And while I know that for anyone born in the past thirty years, this is all completely normal and will remain so forever, I still believe that art and ideas, especially when they're good, deserve to be experienced with a little mystery and imagination. Which is to say, without looking at their creators and wondering why they picked such an ugly shirt or whether they look like a Jay Leno Muppet. We can do that on our own.

– Femcel Cope –
(A Case Against Early Marriage)

March 2024

T hirty years ago, when I was in college, all I wanted was a serious boyfriend. This desire was my greatest shame at the time and has remained a source of self-rebuke ever since, as have many aspects of my character during those four years. The grandiosity of that statement shames me all over again, since by the standards of a lot of undergraduate nincompoopery, I was well within normal limits. But my lack of academic discipline combined with an almost compulsive need to appear more sophisticated than I was meant I spent most of my time holding forth pretentiously about art and culture while never completing

my actual reading assignments. I'd like to say the reason for not completing them was that I was busy playing sports or playing in the orchestra or even partying at fraternity houses. But I'm afraid the real reason was that I was so preoccupied with my own longing that I couldn't concentrate on anything else.

The worst part about this longing was that it was so specific as to preclude actually getting into a relationship. Aside from one man (if you can call a twenty-year-old a man) who was essentially an on-again-off-again friend-with-benefits onto whom I had projected a set of fictions of which I could not disabuse myself despite relentless evidence to the contrary, no one at the college interested me romantically. Looking back on it now, I don't see how there could have been. The campus was populated with roughly 2,300 students, all between the ages of eighteen and twenty-two. Even if females hadn't vastly outnumbered the males and even if a good portion of the males hadn't been gay, this college would not have been a useful mating pool for a young lady in want of a husband.

Not that I wanted a husband. I wanted a studio apartment with a futon on which I might fall asleep in the loving embrace of a broad-chested, scratchy-faced individual in possession of a bachelor's degree and at least one sport coat and tie, if not a job to go along with them. I wanted not to be in college but to live in New York City and on my way to doing exciting and maybe even important things and I wanted this broad-chested person to wear his sport coat to meet after work in a midtown bar, where we would eat calamari and talk about our respective days before going back to one of our apartments and watching a rented movie from Blockbuster.

I wanted to be an adult with an adult relationship. I also sort of wanted to have children, but mostly because I was not able to see 'adult relationship' as a separate organ from the nuclear family. I wanted to love and be loved by a mature man, and I thought motherhood was simply the price of the ticket. It was the very early nineties, and my chief template for adult relationships was the lead couple on the television show *Thirtysomething.* Michael Steadman and Hope Murdoch Steadman were gorgeous and accomplished and shared semi-equally in the care of their baby daughter. He was a Penn grad and she was a Princeton grad and they were nothing if not the epitome of a hypergamous partnership. The concept of hypergamy, which refers to women preferring mating partners whose education levels and socioeconomic status are equivalent or higher to their own, was not in common use back then, but I and every woman I knew practiced it without a second thought. We didn't date plumbers or electricians. We dated television producers, aspiring professors and advertising agency creatives like Michael Steadman. Actually, that's not quite accurate. We wanted to date those guys, but there weren't enough to go around. So we often dated no one at all.

By the late nineties, the yuppie love ethos of *Thirty-something* had given way to the you-go-girl hookup culture of *Sex and the City*, which eventually devolved into the raunch era marked by franchises like Girls Gone Wild, stripper poles marketed as exercise equipment and twerking presented as an expression of feminist empowerment. Then dawn broke over online pornography, social media, smartphones and dating apps and human sexual relations were never the same again. Within one generation, the concept of approaching someone in a public space and asking for a phone number had gone from a social norm to a potentially punishable offense. Dating no longer involved keeping your antenna up for persons of interest in the real world but putting your photo and biographical details online and seeing what the algorithm had to say about it.

It's shameful and sad that a hyper-promiscuous, childless woman (Taylor Swift), aging and alone with a cat, has become the heroine of a feminist age.

As I write this, in the early days of 2024, a discussion is happening online about whether the one-two punch of the sexual revolution and the women's movement has been a victim of its own success. The rise of the 'trad movement' has social media influencers cosplaying as traditional wives, even homesteaders, and all manner of anti-woke 'thought leaders' calling for a return to old-fashioned family structures.

Sometimes this discourse sounds like an earnest call to fess up to some basic but uncomfortable truths about human behavior and biology. For instance, this: contrary to what second-wave feminism and *Cosmopolitan* magazine told us, lots of women actually do want to settle down and start families relatively young. The fact that this option has been stigmatized by the educated classes is now causing a lot of female misery, not to mention a lot of bad male behavior that's been reclassified as 'treating women like equals'.

At the same time, the economic and social gains afforded to women by the sexual revolution have allowed them to be a lot pickier about their life choices. Some of them legitimately don't want to have children and have arranged their lives accordingly. Some would rather have children without the added responsibility of a childlike male partner, and reproductive technology is making this easier all the time. Others are stewing around in their anger, venting online about male toxicity and gaslighting and, in numbers that beggar belief, identifying as something other than entirely female, which is unlikely to help their dating prospects with entirely male men.

In turn, men are responding as men tend to do, with a combination of exuberance, indifference and primal rage born of humiliation. The ones whose social capital, educational attainment and physical appearance render them 'high value' (the concept of 'mate value' comes from Darwin; don't blame me), are having the time of their lives because there aren't nearly enough of them for all the upwardly mobile women who want them. Others, probably the vast majority, are puttering along, trying to make the best of things and trying even harder to keep their mouths shut.

And then there is a small, extremely online and increasingly noisy group whose 'low value' status has become a self-fulfilling prophecy and made them very angry indeed. In a winner-take-all dating economy, their lonely free time leads them to video games, YouTube and a limitless landscape of pornography, much of it depicting activities no actual human being would ever think or want to do in the real world. They spend money on OnlyFans while reviling the women who earn that money. Along the way, they blame their misery on feminism, obsess about 'body counts' and circulate memes about empty egg cartons and roast beef sandwiches. In case you need a primer, I regret to tell you that body count refers to the number of sexual partners a woman has had and the empty egg carton is a reference to the ovaries of any women over thirty.

Another dog mom crying about men because she hit the wall full speed without building her own loving family. Your opinion is void and empty like your egg carton.

11:54 PM · **15** Views

As for the sandwich, it seems that some men operate on the belief that the more sexual partners a woman has had, the more her labia minora resembles deli meat. I will spare you the visual on that one.

Knowing a business opportunity when they see one, manosphere gurus and 'entrepreneurial space' leaders swoop in and spread a pro-natalist prosperity gospel that becomes its own kind of pornography. While you're busy building wealth through real estate, startup ventures, or cryptocurrency, don't forget to 'wife up' with a woman young and fertile enough to give you the highest ROI (Return On Investment).

Back in the *Sex and the City* era, this sort of thing would have been relegated to radio shock jock banter or post-firewalk rap sessions at mythopoetic men's retreats. It would have been laughed off by women and mocked by men, often while they were all sitting around the same table enjoying themselves. Today, some serious people are taking it very seriously. Not the deli meat stuff (I choose to believe no one over twenty-five takes that seriously) but the dystopic malaise that brought it about. Some very educated, liberal-minded people are talking about the hazards of going it alone, the benefits of marrying young and the existential duty to produce offspring. I myself have participated in these conversations both publicly and privately. I have advised young women to not let go of a good relationship because they mistakenly believe that their prize for professional achievement is access to a pool of 'higher value' men (spoiler: it sometimes works just the opposite). I can tell something has gone very wrong with our mating and dating patterns, with the way we think about sex and try to carry it out, with our whole human project.

I say this while knowing that I am the cautionary tale in the room. I am over fifty and I am childless and alone. I'm not just an empty egg carton. I'm an empty egg carton made from the recycled pulp of multiple generations of tossed-out egg cartons. My original carton was abandoned long ago. If you want to teach young people to grow up, pair up and procreate, I'm a case study in what not to do. Yet I don't regret how things have gone. I can't imagine things going any other way and am actually glad they didn't. I know that's nothing but 'cope' as the kids say online now – 'pure cope', even – but it also happens to be true. It's not that I squandered my opportunities to build a family: I just didn't have the kinds of opportunities that would have made me want to do so. Or maybe I did have those opportunities but for some reason chose to look in the other direction. Maybe I wanted nothing to do with those opportunities, even if they were sitting right before me. And if I didn't want them, wouldn't that suggest that I wasn't meant to have them?

I'd say yes, except for there being a time when I wanted them more than anything else. When I was very young, far too young to know the difference between what I wanted and what I thought I wanted, I desired only to have an adult relationship with my proverbial Michael Steadman. (Surely it was no accident that *Thirtysomething*'s creators had deemed their lead male character a literal steady man.) And insofar as serious people are now entertaining the theory that a twenty-year-old woman who wants nothing more than an adult relationship with a steady, trustworthy provider will fare much better in life if she prioritizes finding a good mate above all else, I am hereby volunteering myself as a lab specimen to test that theory. I am donating my personal romantic history to science, or at least the shoddy social science of literary essays. So let us return to where this essay began.

Less than a week after graduating college, I met a broad-chested Penn grad named Michael and he became my boyfriend for three years. He was eight years older than me and we met at work in a way that I suspect wouldn't be possible now, which is to say he was in a senior position and I was an entry-level assistant and he asked me to lunch and then to dinner and within a month we were meeting up in midtown bars after work, drinking cocktails, enjoying the occasional shared cigarette and sometimes ordering calamari. Then we'd go back to his studio co-op, order Chinese food and watch a movie or, if it was a Monday night, *Northern Exposure*, a show about a young Jewish doctor in Alaska named Joel Fleischman. At the end of that summer, Michael turned thirty, which freaked me out, since by now we were officially a couple and I was only twenty-two.

Still, I thought Michael was the smartest, funniest, most cultured man I'd ever met. He was short and sometimes wore ill-fitting dockers with his sport coats, but I thought he was handsome and sexy in a Joel Fleischman sort of way. As it happened, Michael loved *Thirtysomething* as much as I did and even though the show had been canceled the year before, we spent a lot of time talking about the characters and analyzing the storylines. This lent a meta quality to the whole relationship, as if I were living in some proto version of the television show on which I had modeled my life. At night, we'd lie in bed and Michael would explain Keynesian economics and sometimes I'd ask questions in a silly little girl voice that started out as a joke but maybe took hold a little too much. He made me watch all the movies I needed to see and read all the books I needed to read. *Jesus' Son* by Denis Johnson. *Black Tickets* by Jayne Anne Phillips. Norman Mailer's *Advertisements For Myself.* We both knew the dialogue from several Woody Allen movies from memory and we'd often dip into moments of reenactment, tossing out lines like 'I happen to have Marshall McLuhan right here' when some nearby blowhard was getting his name-dropping all wrong.

I couldn't believe my luck. I also couldn't believe my bad timing. Michael was thirty and thinking about marriage. I was twenty-two and would have been mortified to settle down so young. If I'd even considered such a thing, my friends would have surely held an intervention. They liked him well enough, but let's be real: I had miles to go before I slept. I was talking about quitting my job and going to grad school. I was proselytizing about this new obscure indie band called the Dave Matthews Band. I was hanging out with roommates in a gritty apartment way uptown, watching *The Real World* on MTV and drinking vodka out of coffee mugs when there were no clean glasses. My friends would have told me not to cash in my chips at the first adult relationship out of the gate. And they would have been right. By the second year with Michael, I could feel myself outgrowing him. It wasn't that I loved him any less. I was just aging past him, as if he were the *Complete Stories of Kurt Vonnegut* and I'd just discovered Thomas Pynchon. By the third year I was having nightmares in which I was trapped on a city bus that was careening past the expected stops and headed somewhere I was pretty sure I didn't want to go. I pulled the cord again and again to signal the driver, but no chime rang out.

One weekend afternoon, after a tumultuous few months of 'trial separation' followed by a lackluster six weeks of 'getting back together' (wherein Michael wondered aloud when we would get married) I mustered the courage to take the subway down to his apartment and end things for good. The whole tear-soaked scene lasted less than fifteen minutes. I told him I knew I could never marry him. The combination of guilt, sorrow and fear added up to what was probably the worst I'd felt ever about anything in my life up to that point.

I was so shaken that I indulged in a taxi to take me the eighty blocks north to my apartment. In a move that is either completely badass or utterly ridiculous depending on your perspective, I asked the driver to stop at a bodega and leave the meter running while I ran in for a pack of cigarettes. He obliged, as if it was nothing out of the ordinary, and when I returned I asked if I could smoke in the cab and he said sure. So I rolled down the window and smoked all the way uptown. In so doing I transformed into someone different from the person who'd come downtown not half an hour before. I became someone who smoked in cabs. Not literally, since I never did it again, but figuratively for sure.

From there commenced a solid decade of figurative cab smoking. The year after Michael, I bleached my hair white, started wearing baby doll dresses with Doc Martin boots, and spent the next two-and-a-half years serially monogamizing my way through people who ranged from somewhat inappropriate (still living in ex's apartment) to highly inappropriate (wanted by the law). Though I suspect I was fairly miserable at the time, I now look back fondly on this period, mostly because it was when I finally managed to get an apartment without roommates. When I was twenty-eight, I got dumped by a long-distance paramour who was laughably wrong for me but whom I'd convinced myself was my unlikely soul mate (reader, he lived in *Florida* and was a *Republican*) and spent ten days crying on the couch, lighting one American Spirit cigarette after the other.

What was wrong with me? I didn't really want to get married, but I did want someone to go out for Indian food with and lie in bed with on weekend mornings reading *The New York Times*. For some reason, this person was not materializing. Now and then I'd go out to dinner with a handsome investment banker who would do things like walk me twenty blocks back to my apartment, come up to 'borrow a book' and then immediately leave.

I was also going increasingly broke during this time, my career advancements running in inverse proportion to my actual ability to pay my bills. At some point after my twenty-ninth birthday, I became consumed by the notion that I should move to Lincoln, Nebraska. I had been there on a reporting assignment the year before and it had ignited the *Little House On*

The Prairie fantasies that had lain dormant in me since childhood. The move was mostly to lower my cost of living but also kind of because I wanted to meet different sorts of men, though I would never have admitted as much. So I packed up my stuff, bought a one-way ticket on TWA and flew off to my next incarnation.

Within three days of arriving in Nebraska, I went jogging in the woods and met a bearded wildman who was sitting alone by a campfire reading poetry. He asked for my phone number and within five months we were living in a 500-square-foot bungalow with a lopsided porch on twelve acres outside of town; an actual little house on the prairie. From there ensued two years of more chaos and absurdity than I can go into here, but suffice it to say I went even more broke thanks in part to the wildman's eccentricities and substance abuse.

This would have been a disaster had I not managed to fictionalize the whole situation and turn it into a novel that sold for enough money to allow me to move to Los Angeles. Upon arriving there, I promptly began dating a guy who had a nice apartment and a steady job but who I only seemed to like when I was not in his presence. This resulted in confusion that caused me to do several things I would later deeply regret, and I came to hate myself even more than I hated him. After that relationship ended, I didn't date anyone for well over a year. When I got back in the game, I briefly tried online dating but was so mortified by the idea of advertising myself as someone who wanted a boyfriend that I deleted my account in less than a month. A short while after that, I joined a group of colleagues for dim sum and met the man who would become my husband and later my ex-husband.

I've written enough about what went wrong in our marriage that it doesn't bear repeating here (I also promised my ex-husband I would never write about him again), but suffice it to say that I went into marriage hoping I could be a certain kind of person and came out of it accepting that I was never going to be anyone other than what I was. By certain kind of person, I mean a person who didn't need so much time alone, a person who tried new things (like surfing, which my husband wanted me to try harder at), a person who was more enthusiastic about family life than I was ever going to be. Also, a person who skied. I am convinced to this day that at least half of my relationships, including the one with Michael, ended in part because I don't ski.

For a long time, my failure to be a certain kind of person, namely one that wanted to raise a family, made me feel very bad. But given that I was raised in a family that had been established primarily as a statement of opposition to the families from which it sprang, I don't see how I could have turned out any differently. Both of my parents, for different reasons, denounced where they had come from. As far as they were concerned, they had no pasts, no childhoods.

They had each entered the world fully formed and catching the next Greyhound bus out of their small southern-Midwest towns. As such, they created not a family but an island comprised of four individuals with no ties to anyone but each other. This might have been okay if we liked each other more. But as it was, we were a sad little unit that actively decried the importance of extended family. Getting together with relatives was for rubes. Or at least our relatives were rubes, so it was lucky for us that we never saw them. As I grew older, it was made clear that things like dating, marrying and procreating fell into the same category as attending family reunions and owning a camper: it was the breakfast of Philistines.

By the time I was in my teens, the island was eroding along the edges. My father's eccentricities were shaping up to be professional and economic liabilities. Despite ferocious talent, he seemed unable to imagine anything beyond a hand-to-mouth financial existence. He earned as much money as he needed to earn, and not a penny more. In response, my mother embarked on a new career and adopted an entirely new personality to go along with it. When they finally split up, they remained married, partly because my father needed my mother's health insurance and partly because divorcing would have implied that either of them took seriously the prospect of forming new relationships. In the end, my mother never had another romantic relationship, at least that I knew of. My father had a series of relationships with women who enjoyed his company but were otherwise unavailable in one way or another, including being married to other people. His last relationship lasted several years and thrived in no small part because he and his girlfriend kept separate homes in different boroughs of New York City. My father never loved anyplace, or possibly any person, more than he loved the island of Manhattan.

My father rose to the occasion of family life as best he could, but I'm confident he would have been better off on his own. He more or less admitted as much, telling my brother and me that he was glad he had us but that he was the kind of person who never should have married and had children. I've always admired the honesty of that statement, just as I resented my mother's decades-long effort to fit the square peg of her husband into the round hole of whatever idea she had about how life was supposed to go.

I knew it was wrong to resent her. If anything, I should have begrudged him for his recalcitrance and admired her for trying so hard for so long. But I am my father's daughter. It turns out that I, too, am the kind of person who should never marry or have children. I used to joke that by not procreating, I was fulfilling my father's unrealized dreams. It's a great joke that's made all the better for being completely serious. I once asked my father how he'd feel about being a grandfather. He shook his head and said, 'I guess I'd get used to it eventually.'

Neither my brother nor I have children. We have broken off our branch of the family tree. My brother's feelings about this are not mine to share, but my feeling is that this is for the best. Unless you count my dog, I am alone on my own island. As far as I'm concerned, the only downside is the financial strain of being entirely self-supporting. I have no money other than what I earn. I have no one to look after my dog when I travel, so I have to pay for expensive boarding. I have no one to drive me to the airport, so I have to shell out hundreds of dollars to either park in the long-term lot or take taxis or Ubers. As I grow older and eventually infirm, I will have no one to drive me to medical appointments or help me around the house, so I'll have to outsource this work, which will be costly and demoralizing. Nonetheless, I'm pretty certain I'm living my best life, by which I mean the life that was charted for me by some combination of the fates and my own weird temperament. I have meaningful work and good friends and a boyfriend-sized dog who refuses to sleep in the bed but whose snoring from the floor beside me is a sweet soporific. Every morning, the dog wakes me up by placing an enormous paw on the pillow next to my head. As annoying as I sometimes find this, I know that getting up and taking care of a child every morning would be an existential catastrophe by comparison. People always say 'no one ever wakes up every morning and thinks "thank God I don't have kids".' As it happens, I do.

Do I wish I came from another sort of family? Sure. Most people do. But I feel I did the best I could with what I had to work with. Not that someone else couldn't have done a lot better with the same materials. I often wonder how things might have gone had the contours of our family been different. I wonder what would have happened if there had been a third sibling, which my mother always wanted but claimed my father forbade, whatever that means. (Actually, I know what it means, and I'll leave it at that.) Would that child, raised in the same household but with a different psychological profile, have processed the world differently? Would they have taken all that desert island energy and converted it into a fertile plain? Would they have committed the ultimate act of rebellion and married young and produced a houseful of kids? Would I have nieces and nephews now? Would my parents have had grandchildren? Would they have enjoyed those grandchildren in addition to getting used to them? Or would they have been mildly embarrassed by the whole thing?

You could argue that these are pointless questions, since the presence of a third sibling would have changed the family dynamic in such a way that it was a different family altogether. But in our case, I don't think that's true. There could have been ten of us kids or we could have lived in France or been Inuit in an igloo and my father was never going to be anything other than what he was. My mother was more malleable and could have been a lot of different things depending on who she married and where she lived. But she was always going to be irremediably damaged by where she came from. She was always going to be someone who, when I was in my thirties and safely out of child bride territory, told me it was wonderful that I was single but that she wouldn't mind seeing me 'try marriage' someday.

Still, I wonder how I got here. What parts of my island existence are the result of cognitive hardwiring and which came about because of choice or circumstance? What if I'd gone to a large university filled with athletes and engineering majors rather than a small liberal arts college filled with hair gel and cocaine? Would I have found love by age twenty-two and married at twenty-five? Would I have been unencumbered by the cultural baggage that told me young marriage was uncool? (Unlikely, since my parents were part of that particular luggage set.) What if I'd had the same relationship with Michael but was in a social circle where people got married in their early twenties? Would I have married him within that first year and a half, while I was still lolling about in my *Thirtysomething* fantasy? Would the reality of that commitment have precluded the dreams about buses speeding past their stops? Would my young brain have had the neuroplasticity to allow me to grow into a *certain kind of person*? Or were my neurons programmed for cab smoking from the start?

In 2014, around the time my marriage was officially coming apart, a woman named Susan Patton published a ham-handed but unforgettable editorial in the Princeton student newspaper. In it, she urged the female students there to be less ambitious about their future careers and more focused on finding their future husbands. 'You will never again have this concentration of men who are worthy of you,' she wrote.

Patton was not a student, but a 1970s-era graduate of the university with a son currently enrolled at Princeton (lucky him!). The letter became a viral sensation and Patton, who was instantly and permanently dubbed The Princeton Mom, became a pariah, scorned by snarky media feminists and of course given a book deal.

I was one such feminist. I was a newspaper columnist then and wrote that Patton's position was driven less out of genuine concern than by class anxiety and

her own self-rebuke for having married a man from a
lesser school – from whom she was recently divorced.
I doubt I was wrong about that, but even at the time I
knew Patton's core message was right. Princeton may
have had a more balanced male/female ratio in 2014
than in Hope Murdoch's time, but for most of the
female undergraduates, this was about as fertile a mating ground as they were likely to find in their lifetimes,
as least in terms of sheer numbers. That vanishingly
few of those male undergraduates would have had any
incentive to pick a partner at that stage in life seemed
a minor detail. For Patton, it was all about not letting
good minds go to waste, even if most of those minds
were attached to bodies that were playing beer pong
and passing out in the bushes.

'If you associate too closely with a man who is sig-
nificantly below your intellectual level,' Patton wrote
in her book, 'you will eventually get stupid juice all
over you.'

In an alternate version of my life, I don't go to the artsy
liberal arts college but to an enormous state university. I go to school in Wisconsin or Massachusetts or
Texas and it's less like going to college than like being
eighteen-years-old and moving to a new town on my
own. Maybe I live in a dorm for one semester or the
first year and maybe it's the kind of sterile high-rise
tower that, in my actual life, seemed to defeat the
whole purpose of going to college. (The purpose being

that you should feel like you're in a movie about going to college; this required red brick buildings and ivy.) But after that, I move off-campus, take a part-time job and live like an adult. I go to classes but mostly I write for the campus newspaper or play in the orchestra or throw myself into some kind of activity that fosters close, lifelong friends. (In the alternate version of my life, I play the violin rather than the oboe.)

Maybe I meet a serious romantic partner (chances are good; since there are tens of thousands of students on campus) and maybe we set up house in a ramshackle bungalow filled with houseplants and thrift shop furniture. Maybe this person elicits not only love and affection but also a sense of liking myself more when I'm in his presence. Maybe this person is a boyishly handsome public interest lawyer whom I both respect and admire. And maybe because I am in Madison or Amherst or Austin surrounded by normal people rather than gorgeous, neurotic elites from Park Avenue who I'm trying in vain to emulate, I don't automatically assume that settling down early is a total rube thing to do. Maybe I find it in me to quit while I'm ahead and forge a life with this person. And maybe by cutting myself off at the pass, I become *a certain kind of person* by process of elimination. Maybe despite the sour influence of my parents, I have a beautiful – or at least beautiful enough – life with this person, a life with children and relatives and family vacations and all the things that are enjoyed by people who aren't me, by which I mean the me that I turned out to be.

But when does that path begin? Are you on it before you can even walk? Does the path precede you, like pavement laid in a past life?

The night I knew I had to break up with Michael was a night I went to a raucous dinner party in a rambling old apartment near Columbia University, where I was by then in graduate school. The rooms echoed with the loud laughter of worldly intellectuals joking about whatever people used to joke about back then. There was homemade Persian food and Miles Davis playing on the stereo and bottle after bottle of seven dollar Merlot. After dinner, everyone sat around a long table smoking cigarettes and pouring more wine and laughing harder and harder as they got drunker. I remember feeling like this scene was the embodiment of everything I wanted my life to be. It was a scene that was the opposite of anything having to do with Michael, though I couldn't quite put my finger on why, since he was smart and funny and capable of eating Persian food and even smoking after dinner. It would be several more months before I smoked that cigarette in the cab after going to his apartment to break his heart, but our relationship effectively died that evening.

What if I'd married him before going to that dinner party? What if I'd never gone to the dinner party at all? What if I'd gone to the state school and met

Michael there? Would I have liked him as much? Or was part of my enchantment with him that he was so different from the men of the effete liberal arts college? What if I'd met the boyishly handsome public interest lawyer not in Madison or Amherst or Austin but in New York City, after graduating from the effete college? Would I have still settled down with him early? Or would we be just another stop on our respective serial monogamy trains? Or are these moot questions, since the New York City dating economy is such that he'd be dating the proverbial supermodel who also happens to have a PhD and would never look my way? (I'll wager a yes.)

In an alternate version of my life following my divorce when I'm forty-five, I mope around for a few months and then meet my absolute perfect match. This man's vocation has nothing to do with my own. He is a cancer researcher or a particle physicist or the principal cellist in the London Philharmonic. He is among the top in his field and an utter workaholic whose marriage broke up because he wouldn't take vacations and never saw his kids. We are perfect for each other because I am also a workaholic who hates vacations and, better yet, I have no kids at all. This man will be no more than three years younger or no more than ten years older than me. He will be a grizzled silver hair type with the body of an aging jock, though he won't actually do any jock activities, at least none that would involve me. Maybe this man used to ski but now has bad knees and now just sea kayaks occasionally. We see each other on alternate weekends and probably don't even live in the same city.

Why would any man be interested in marriage with a 52 year old empty egg carton?

In the actual version of my life following my divorce, I met a few men like this, then realized they almost exclusively dated women decades younger. Since I was once a young woman dating older men (though not by decades) I was in no position to complain, but nor was I willing to assume my rightful place in the mating economy and date septuagenarians. Over the next six years, I had exactly three relationships you might call romantic. Most were shortlived and none serious, though let the record show that the men were grizzled, athletic types relatively close to my own age. Out of the three, only one had an actual job. It wasn't as a world-famous cancer researcher. As I write this, I have had no romantic life for going on two years. This is definitely for lack of trying. You've heard of incels; I am a vol-cel. My body count is holding steady.

In the alternate version of my life before I'm even born, I have the DNA of someone who can happily grow old with another person. I am the product of two people who enjoy the presence of children and who like their own families and maybe even like themselves. I have a completely different set of values, skills and interests – I can ski! – and these things lend themselves to coexisting happily alongside others. I don't need too much alone time and my tastes in everything from food to music to romantic partners is broad enough that I embrace the world with open arms and there's a wide range of people that I find sexually attractive. Maybe I do the thing I now fantasize about and become a federal investigator, busting human traffickers and wearing pantsuits that, thanks to my DNA, look sleek even with a gun in a hip holster. Maybe I'm good at math so I go into finance and live comfortably and take exotic vacations on which I try new things and have fun. Maybe I find a partner at a young age and have a big family and we grow old together in rocking chairs surrounded by our progeny. Or maybe the universe cuts me off at the pass before that can even happen. Maybe I die in a car wreck when I'm sixteen or in my crib when I'm six months. Or maybe since I went into finance I'm in one of the towers on 9/11. And maybe I jump to my death because I have the DNA of someone who would jump rather than someone who would cover her face with her hands and wait to die.

In the actual version of my life before I'm even born, the two people who would become my mother and father have struggles I will never know the half of. Those struggles are partly the result of the struggles of the people who became their parents and, of course, the struggles of the people before them. There is poverty and illness. There are talents and deficiencies. There is love and apathy. There are family secrets that are either too dark or too dull to be mentioned anymore than in passing. The inner worlds of the two people who become my parents will mostly elude me, despite a lifetime of dissecting them in therapists' offices and trying to put them into words on paper. These two people will die being grateful for some things and regretful about other things and I will have only the faintest grasp of what those things are. I will feel sad for them that they don't have grandchildren. I will feel this sadness even though I honestly don't think they were all that sad about it themselves. But I feel sad nonetheless. I feel sad not about what we didn't have but what we could never bring ourselves to want.

*

Do you know what are the most common last words of the childless as they lay in their deathbed?

Nobody does. Because they're all alone.

8:45 PM · **1.2M** Views

Grief is everywhere. I still grieve the end of my marriage, even seven years after the fact. I grieve the deaths of my parents. In some ways I grieve their lives, too. I grieve for what might have been had they not been damaged in the ways that they were damaged. I know they grieved similarly for their own parents. My father never knew his father. His mother didn't finish high school until her forties. My mother's mother was a sickly child and missed entire years of school, leaving her suspended in a childlike state that my mother likened to an intellectual disability. I never asked her to elaborate on that. Talking about their families caused my parents so much anguish that I avoided the subject out of a certain compassion.

Cope is everywhere. The more years you're alive, the greater percentage of your day is taken up by cope. Eventually, it just becomes the default setting. You needn't call attention to it any more than you'd need to point out that your heart is beating. *Cope harder*, the kids might taunt. Well, sorry, the dial is already up to eleven. Besides, what's the opposite of cope? Carrying your regrets like a pocketknife and lacerating yourself whenever one crosses your mind? Is it cope to say that in the thirty-plus years since those college days of longing for love, there wasn't a single man (or woman) in my romantic orbit who could have made my life any happier than it is now? Is it cope to blame this on factors beyond my control, like genetics and sad family dynamics, rather than on my inability or unwillingness to move past those factors?

There are no answers to these questions. The trad influencers and bro-tech boys may think they have the answers now. But as they get older, those answers will slough away like dead skin. A thirty-year-old woman I know, married with a child, recently joked to me that my life was her biggest nightmare. She wasn't actually joking, but it struck me as funny nonetheless. I'm glad for her sake that she's wired differently than I am. But I'm even gladder for my own sake that one person's nightmare can be another's nonpareil. When I was thirty, I was living in a tiny farmhouse with a man who was half mad, furiously trying to write my way out of the chaos I'd put myself in. If you'd given me a peek at the life I have today and offered me an escape portal directly to this chair in which I now sit, surrounded by books and art and with a dog lying at my feet, I would have taken it in a heartbeat. I would have taken it when I was forty-two and miserable in my marriage and maybe even when I was twenty-five and smoking in that cab – though I would have requested a return ticket; the trip would have been strictly exploratory.

But I would not have taken it when I was twenty or twenty-two or even twenty-four. Back then, I longed for a life that was all wrong for me, a life that was never going to be compatible with my brain chemistry or my hobbies or interests or lack thereof. If I'd somehow been granted that life, I might have been happy for a while, possibly even for a long time. But I am all but certain that this alternate version of me would have aged into someone who had her nose pressed against the glass of the actual version of me.

I know this because sometimes I see her watching me from a distance. She is the young mother with her small daughter in the park, staring into the distance and noticing, for a drawn-out moment, a middle-aged woman sitting with her dog on the grass a hundred feet or so away. She is the wife dining with her husband in a restaurant, scanning the room and fixing her gaze on a woman reading a book as she eats alone at the bar. The world may want her to pity these solo travelers, but I can feel her approval, even her envy, as acutely as if it were my own. It is my own. She is the alternate me, a woman living a good life that is also the wrong life. She is a woman whose life is a slightly ill-fitting garment. It has never draped quite right across the contours of her soul. Her life is arguably better than that of the lone woman, but there will always be a part of her that wants nothing more than to sit quietly on the grass with her dog, away from the playground, away from the main dining room. I know the story is supposed to end with me saying the same about her, but I can't. I have no wish to be her. I am in the right life. How did I get so lucky?

– The Catastrophe Hour –

April 2024

In the summer of 2017 I bought a 9,500-square-foot parcel of land in the foothills of northeast Los Angeles with the intent to build a modest house on it. All modesty aside, this is a next-level insane thing to do, but I have always been insane about real estate and I guess I wanted to level up in that department. In fact, it was the recognition of my own insanity that led me to the belief that spending several years and tens of thousands of dollars drawing plans, securing permits, battling neighborhood councils and paying for costly reports from surveyors, civil engineers, structural engineers, state certified arborists and geological inspectors before taking out a monstrous construction loan would be better for my mental health than trying to buy an existing house in the normal way.

At that time, the median home price in Los Angeles County was around $800,000. Since 'median' doesn't really tell you anything, it would be more accurate to say that the average two-bedroom, one-bathroom house in the northeast LA neighborhoods that I consider home (more expensive at the time than certain suburbs but cheaper than many other places in the city) was selling for an average of $800,000. Final sale prices were nearly always well over the original asking price, often with multiple cash offers. Effectively that meant that if I wanted to purchase an 800-square-foot house in decent shape in a neighborhood with which I had any familiarity I'd need at least $875,000 cash.

Having something much less than that, my idea was to buy a parcel of land with the cash I did have, hire an architect who was also a trusted friend and slowly begin preparations on a tastefully minimalist home that I was told shouldn't cost more than $300 per square foot to build. In other words, even if it went massively over budget (which it definitely would) I would still be able to get financing on a construction loan and come out in the end with a house worth far more than what I'd put into it. Even if the place was rendered unaffordable thanks to mortgage, insurance and property taxes, I could put it on the market and make enough of a profit to buy the aforementioned 800-square-foot house in decent shape in a neighborhood I didn't hate. Never mind that the attendant financial panic would likely shave years off my life. I was, as I took to saying, 'ready to have my life ruined by something else for a change.'

What had been ruining my life up until that point? Everything and nothing. Like most fifty-somethings with too many blessings to count, most of what was bad about my life took the form of either encroaching bodily decrepitude (in the span of a few months, the skin above my knees had appeared to loosen itself from the muscle and bone nearly completely and take on the qualities of crepe paper) or negative stimulation via social media. According to the helpful screen time monitor on my MacBook, I spent an average of ten hours a day online.

I told myself that this was due to overwork, but the truth was that probably half of it was wasted on Twitter (the site formerly known as Twitter, now X. Or, as I call it, Twitterx). Most of what I saw there was nothing more than an algorithmic reflection of my own biases and obsessions. The machine knew where I clicked, what I lingered on, and delivered a steady flow of dopamine, much of it in the form of culture war content, which apparently I continue to be obsessed with despite having written and published a book about the culture wars that effectively broke my brain.

Like most terms bobbing along the surface of public conversation these days, 'culture war' is vague to the point of uselessness. But suffice it to say that my concerns about things like Covid origins, narrowing definitions of womanhood and a certain overlap between extreme leftist activism and narcissistic personality disorder had compressed my Twitter timeline into something akin to a blocked artery. I saw very little other than expressions of outrage at other people's outrage. Libs of TikTok, The Babylon Bee, any number of parody accounts lampooning virtue signaling liberals; it was the atherosclerosis interrupting the blood flow of a natural life. On my own podcasts (somehow I'd ended up hosting not one but two podcasts devoted to Fighting Groupthink) I banged on about gender and leftist overreach week after week. Meantime, back in the physical world – the realm of 'touching grass', as they said in the Twitterxsphere – I took a low dose statin to keep my real arteries from clogging any further and obsessed about the skin around my knees. I couldn't believe how old I'd become.

Had I bought an existing house in 2017 for $800,000, it would easily be worth $1.3 million today. Alternatively, had I been able to get underway with my construction project in 2017 and finish it by 2019, I would have spent around $600,000 to build something that would be worth close to $1.6 million right now. Instead, I spent two and a half years obtaining permits, navigating a labyrinthine zoning department and paying for not only architectural plans but geological surveys, sewer permits, street improvement clearances, an inventory of 'California protected trees' performed by a state-licensed arborist, and, most of all, fighting a mentally unhinged neighbor who mobilized the entire block against me on the pretense that I had to build a sidewalk in front of my house even though the entire neighborhood is composed of craggy hillsides and there are no sidewalks anywhere.

Then the pandemic came. Everything stopped for the better part of two years. By the time the bureaucratic gears began turning again, the strangulated supply chain had sent the price of lumber into the stratosphere, from whence it will never come back down. The national housing boom drove subcontractors out of California and into states like Texas, where fewer regulations meant houses were being built faster and cheaper, resulting in years-long waits for competent roofers and carpenters. By the time the Fed raised interest rates in 2022, my mid-six-figure project had turned into a seven-figure project. Along the way, my income had dipped into a fraction of its former self, restoring the adjusted gross income on my tax returns to a number I hadn't seen since my twenties. Not only was I nowhere close to qualifying for a seven-figure construction loan, my anxiety level all but guaranteed a coronary event if I attempted the project.

So in the summer of 2023, exactly seven years after purchasing it, I put the whole kaboodle on the market: architectural plans, permits, clearances, surveys, reports; all of it. That meant I could go on Zillow and look at an AI-assisted rendering of my dream house, a minimalist barn-style structure that, as with most of my creative projects, doesn't exactly appeal to the masses. I knew it would likely take a year or more to sell and, even then, I'd be lucky to get a price that recouped my overall financial investment, let alone all that time in Zoning Administration meetings.

In the pantheon of bad choices, the attempt to build my own house towers above all others. I have lost money in LA real estate, which practically defies the laws of physics.

*

Over time, I have come to see my failed construction project as the ultimate metaphor for my life and times. I couldn't just do things the normal way, so I made them a hundred times harder than they needed to be. Then, on top of everything else, the world changed in more ways than anyone could have anticipated. In the case of my career, the written word faded into near obsolescence, reducing my once-respectable pay grade to something rivaling the proceeds from a child's lemonade stand. In the case of building my house, the cascading effects of Covid-19 moved the needle of feasibility from 'crazy idea but, hey, you do you' to 'not gonna happen in your lifetime'. It was, as the kids say, an epic fail.

If the fail didn't involve real estate, I might be able to move past it, or at least foresee a time when the subject doesn't reduce me to a puddle of seething self-rebuke. But the thing is, I care about where I live more than I care about most things at this point. I care about having a beautiful house more than I care about professional success, my physical appearance or having an intimate relationship. If someone showed me the perfect house and said you can either have this or never have sex again in your entire life, I'm pretty sure I'd choose the house without a thought.

Mistakes supply the only lessons that stick. Two doors down from my plot of land is a house that I should have bought in 2017. The house was about 750 square-feet, with a kitchen so small that it had been outfitted with a customized extra narrow refrigerator. There were two bedrooms, only one of which was large enough for a two-person bed. The washer and dryer were outside on the back patio. There was no central air conditioning, which was an extra problem because it appeared that most of the windows were the kind that don't actually open. Still, it was a sexy house. There's no other word for it. It sat on a double lot at the end of a cul-de-sac at the top of a hill, canyonland spilling out from all directions. The rooms may have been small but they were also airy and bright, with a grid pane-picture window taking up most of one living-room wall and built-in bookcases lining the other.

I happened to have had my soon-to-be ex-husband with me when I went to look at the house. We'd been separated for two years and I'd been living in New York. But since I'm never not looking for houses in Los Angeles, I'd wound up with an appointment to see the place, arranged by our long-suffering real estate broker, who knew I was in town. I can't recall exactly why my husband was there, but I do know that I'd gone to his house to sign our divorce papers (we'd been dragging our feet, but now he had a girlfriend and was newly motivated) and we'd gone out to lunch afterward. And now we stood in the little house in the canyon, our longtime broker probably shaking her head at our ceaseless co-dependence (she knew more about our marriage than most people), the summer heat beating down on the flat roof.

'I want this place,' I said. 'I'm making an offer.'

'This house is so small,' my husband said, 'that if you buy it you will never have a relationship ever again.'

'I don't care,' I said.

The house had a list price of, let's just say, *an amount*. (I'm not going to give the actual price because it might be triggering for my readers in the way body weight numbers are triggering for anorexics, by which I really mean that the price is triggering for me.) The broker suggested offering $50k more than that, which I did. When the seller countered at yet another $50k above that, I balked. *That amount* for a 750-square-foot house? Are you crazy? At that price, I won't have any money left to install central air conditioning, let alone ever do a renovation to make it larger.

Five years later, the 750-square-foot house would sell again for nearly twice the price. I have never forgiven myself. Nor have I had a serious romantic relationship since the divorce.

Of course I haven't. The kind of energy that many people put into pursuing sex and romance I put into looking at, thinking about, and occasionally attempting to buy real estate. I look at online listings with the self-loathing compulsion of a pornography addict looking at PornHub. I know my habit is unhealthy and I hate myself for it. But there I am, again and again, refreshing the page to see if a new listing has popped up in the last ten minutes, doing deranged mathematical calculations in which I hope to arrive at a different answer than the correct one, which is that I am nowhere near being able to afford a house in Los Angeles. As of this writing, the median home price in Los Angeles is close to a million dollars.

Just typing that sentence fills me with a despair I can only liken to the despair of heartbreak. As for the obvious question, *why don't you move someplace more affordable?*, answering it makes me feel like a spurned lover, crazed with jealousy and incapacitated by longing. I know I sound like a recalcitrant toddler, but here it is: I don't want to live anywhere else. I have tried to live in other places and have in fact spent many years living in other places. Yet there has not been a single time that my plane has touched down in Los Angeles that I haven't felt a deep sense of coming home. I was born in California (we left when I was three, but a birthplace is a birthplace) and it feels right that I should die here. But I want to die in a house of my own. And the thought that I might not be able to kind of makes me want to die right now.

Enter the catastrophe hour. Every day around 5 p.m. it sets upon me, as reliable as the blue-tinted California skies at the approach of dusk. Every day at this time, unless I happen to be ensconced in some other activity, I begin to hyperventilate just a little. I see time unspooling before me, like a roll of curling ribbon spilled out onto the floor. I gaze upon the walls of my rental house, which are splotched with dog drool that I've been too lazy to wipe off, and suddenly feel that they're closing in around me.

Some days I feel so anxious that the only relief is to go running in 90-degree heat. I think I can sweat out the existential dread, but I'm mostly just losing electrolytes. Some weekends, after running, I go to open houses, 'just to get a sense of the market' and know that this is what it must be like to be a sex addict and to pay for a blow job beneath an overpass. If online real estate listings are pornography, open houses are the logical next step, flesh and blood sex workers, unattainable bodies that hate you back, even if you love them. Stepping across the threshold, the rush is intoxicating. *Could I live here? Could I win the bidding war against the competing offers? Could I drink coffee at this breakfast nook every morning for the rest of my life?* But the moment I get back in my car, I hate myself for what I've done. I've effectively opened a scab and made my wound even worse. What is the wound, you ask? It's the home-shaped hole in my heart.

For most of my life, when I looked at houses for sale, I looked for joy. I surveyed the rooms and imagined myself entertaining houseguests and throwing parties. I imagined myself cooking meals in gleaming kitchens, even though I rarely cook. Now, I picture myself dying in the house. I imagine the whole end-of-life scene; a hospital bed near a window, a bathroom within a few steps, medication bottles crowding the nightstand. I imagine spending my final months (or, if I'm really on the ball, my final year) getting my affairs in order. I'd like to say that means organizing my manuscripts and making sure whatever's left of my money is going to the right people or places. (My mother, who died after a year-long illness, did an outstanding job of this.) But, if I'm honest, 'getting my affairs in order' feels like another way to say 'destroying the evidence'.

What that evidence is, I'm not sure. I just know that the thought of leaving behind the detritus of my life for others to sift through fills me with more terror than the thought of death itself. From time to time, I wake up in the morning and wonder what it would be like to simply purge everything that very day, leaving only a thin, clean layer of basic necessities, nothing that would embarrass if I happened to die in a car crash on the way home from my next trip to the supermarket. This is how the next house will be, I tell myself. Practically empty, so spare that it echoes. By my next house I mean my last house, the house I will die in. I will live there so lightly as to be hardly there at all.

I'm not sure when my house hunting became an extension of end-of-life planning, but I distinctly remember the house that started it. One night in 2019 or so, two chardonnays in and scrolling zombie-like through Zillow, I landed on a sleek, mid-century post and beam in a bland but tony Pasadena neighborhood.

The carport had tandem parking spaces. *That's good*, I thought. *My hospice nurse can park on the left.*

The thought came seemingly out of nowhere. A moment earlier, I'd been thinking about what I was going to eat for dinner. The next, my mind was at death's door, or at least death's carport. The house had several steps leading from the driveway to the front entrance. I studied them closely. Did this obstacle obviate the convenience of the parking space? Would I be able to manage the steps when I was at late-stage whatever I'd die from? Would I need the services of a home health aide in addition to the hospice nurse? Would I be able to afford this aide with whatever I had left of my savings? Would it need to be a burly man who could lift me and carry me up the steps? How much would I weigh? How could I avoid this entire scenario by managing to gently kill myself while I could still manage stairs?

It was a nice looking house. Its price tag was a number composed of four nines and two zeroes. I was still living in New York, but, in my mania, I emailed the long-suffering real estate broker in LA and asked if she thought I stood a chance of buying it if I were able to sell my land. Hypothetically, of course. She wrote back and said that a few years ago I would have had no problem purchasing a house with a 30 percent down-payment but that the market was so hot and financing was so tight that I'd need all cash to buy anything. *Build your house, Meghan*, she said.

Okay, I thought. Fine. Okay. But what about the hospice nurse? My house was designed with two bedrooms in an upstairs loft area. That's no place for a dying woman. Then I remembered there was a den and powder room on the first floor. When I'm dying, I can move to the first floor and my health aide can sleep upstairs, though somehow I'll have to get upstairs to bathe. Unless by then I've carried out my plan to gently kill myself before succumbing to the indignity of a prolonged and painful demise. That said, I shouldn't kill myself in an upstairs bedroom because it might be hard to get my body downstairs. Depending on how much I weigh.

I'd like to tell you that this brand of mordant, mental looky-loo is a very recent development, but I'm afraid this series of thoughts occurred when I was roughly forty-nine years old. My father had died the year before, struck down by a likely pulmonary embolism in the middle of the night when he got up to go to the bathroom. When this occurred, he'd been battling serious health problems, including cancer. Nonetheless, he had never got around to making a will. His affairs were only in order insofar as he'd sold his huge jazz vinyl recording collection a few years earlier.

My father's girlfriend Anne was with him the night he died, which was lucky since even after eight years together they kept separate residences. He could have easily been alone. Anne gave him CPR, or something approaching it, until EMTs from the fire department showed up and, as I later inferred, broke several bones trying to resuscitate him on the floor. It must have been terrible for her, not least because as a non-family member she had no power to tell them to stop when, after twenty minutes, they briefly got back a heartbeat and were ready to transport him to the hospital where he'd be put on life support.

'No no no no no no!' I cried out on the phone to the paramedic. 'Stop! Don't do that!'

So they stopped.

I took an Uber to my father's midtown apartment at 3 a.m., where his body, waxy and colorless, lay on the bed, covered with a blanket. The jolt of it produced an inward gasp that discharged immediately into tears. There were several police officers milling about, taking notes and making reports. They were all extremely kind. The sun rose outside over Second Avenue and eventually the mortuary guys came with a foldable gurney and took my father's body away. It would have to be tilted up vertically to fit in the elevator, a detail I remembered from the removal of my mother's body from her apartment nine years earlier. The officers seemed to be lingering. In our shock, Anne and I kept offering them coffee, which they politely refused. Finally, we realized they were waiting for us to leave.

Because my father had lived there alone and because he was a renter, the apartment door would have to be sealed with police tape and the key taken to the precinct. Apparently this was a New York City law designed to prevent people from looting the apartments of their recently dead neighbors. (Now that I thought of it, I'd seen this tape across the doors of apartments in my own building.) They said the keys would be taken to the police precinct and that I could retrieve them the next day as long as I brought documentation showing I was next of kin.

Because my father had no will, I had no such documentation. Retrieving the key required a probate lawyer and multiple trips to multiple municipal buildings over multiple weeks.

'He was going to get around to making a will,' Anne told me. 'But he wasn't planning on dying anytime soon.'

My father had been a month shy of his seventy-eighth birthday. Had he really not planned on dying? Or was it that drawing up a will felt like overkill? After all, his 'estate' consisted of a couple hundred CDs, a couple of brass musical instruments, some expensive audio equipment and about ten pairs of Jos. A. Bank dress shoes. He had no investments aside from a modest IRA and he certainly didn't own any real estate. My parents had technically been married for forty-two years, the last twenty of which they lived separately and tolerated each other less with every passing year until my mother died. They spent a total of about fifteen years as homeowners, somehow managing to accrue no wealth through this ownership, another gravity-defying feat, given that this time included most of the 1980s.

My mother was obsessed with houses and the beauty of her surroundings. My father saw this as a needless distraction, if not a sign of personal weakness. Left to his own devices, he would have spent his entire adult life happily puttering around in that rent stabilized, one-bedroom apartment in New York City, listening to his CDs and making fun of the personal ads in the *New York Review of Books*. If he had been born in another time and place, he might have skipped the domestic phase altogether, living as a permanent bachelor or, at the very least, a married-without-children urban sophisticate. I have no doubt that this would have been better for him.

I am living my father's best life. That means that when I get semi-resuscitated by paramedics there will probably be no one around to tell them to stop. I'll go straight to the hospital, be put on life support and linger for days in a vegetative state while people figure out whose job it is to give the okay to pull the plug. Not that I don't have an advanced directive. After settling my father's affairs, I hired a lawyer to draw up papers saying the usual stuff about not keeping me alive by artificial means. I printed the papers out and put them in a bright yellow folder marked ADVANCED DIRECTIVE. But the folder is shoved in the back of a cabinet in my office where no one would find it unless they were cleaning out my things because I was already dead.

I made a will, too, of course. I wasn't sure who to leave my plot of land to (it seemed unfair to burden my

147

brother with it; plus he was already getting my retirement account) so I Googled 'best animal charities' and picked a wildlife organization that got high marks from Charity Navigator. I imagined antelope roaming the property as the neighbors peeked over the fence, but I knew I was doing nothing more than tasking my executor with selling the land, which had already proved an impossible feat, and handing over the money so it could be used for God knows what. Speaking of the executor, I could think of no one to do it other than my ex-husband, who accepted the assignment with a combination of amusement and pity. Later I learned you're supposed to pick someone who's younger and likely to be mentally spry enough to handle the duties when the time comes. My ex-husband is one year younger than I am. But he is more physically active than me and his parents are still alive, so I thought I'd take my chances.

I've been told by friends not to talk so much about aging. They say it makes me seem older, the verbal equivalent of a dowdy haircut. I suppose they have a point. Besides, I'm not all that old. I'm not even halfway through my fifties. I may need reading glasses but, curiously, I don't have a strand of grey hair. But being not-old isn't the same as having a long stretch ahead of you. If I live to the age of my mother when she died, I have thirteen years left. If I make it to my father's age, I have twenty-three years. That sounds like a lot until I remember that I still have clothes in my closet that I wore twenty-three years ago. Occasionally I even wear those clothes. Contemplating this makes me want to go directly to my closet and purge of it anything I've had longer than three years, as if I can slow down time by resetting the wardrobe clock.

But then again I want to throw out 90 percent of my possessions anyway. The house I rent is in a little town on the outskirts of Los Angeles, about eight miles from the urban canyon where my land sits. Since receiving the dust-caked contents of the storage locker I emptied out nearly two years ago now, it's only gotten more disorderly. Books lie flat on their sides in piles. Cooking utensils, pet supplies, and stacks of mail spill off the kitchen counters. Every time I take a trip out of town, I imagine what would happen to everything if I never came back. What if my plane crashes or I'm killed on the freeway on the way to the airport? What are people going to do with the contents of my filing cabinets, the boxes of draft manuscripts for books that are both published and not published, the clothes worn and unworn? What will become of the stuff from my parents' cleanouts? The stuff I only kept because throwing it away felt wrong: family photos, my grandmother's jewelry, Christmas stockings, the Lenox wedding china my mother considered too nice to ever actually use?

It will be discarded by someone else. In the end, it hardly matters what you keep and don't keep. Every time you decide to hold onto something, you're mostly just kicking the can down the road. You're deciding to throw it away later – or leave it for someone else to throw away (or to take to Goodwill, where chances are a third party will throw it away). Lately, I can't open my dresser drawers or my medicine cabinet without imagining someone rifling through them because I've died. It's a mortification just to contemplate. It's also a kind of marvel. A living organism can cease to exist in a thousand different ways, but inanimate objects live forever. In the blink of an eye, the contents of my bathroom alone could become a museum. A bottle of expired antibiotics, a travel case that I bought ten years ago and used once, the tweezers in my medicine cabinet; they could easily outlive me. If I die in a car accident tomorrow, the bath towel I used today will be hanging where I left it.

Life loses value over time. The older we get, the less tragic our deaths. Almost everything in our midst loses value. Food spoils, materials break down, world records are beaten. Inflation sends the dollar to the cheap seats. Technology lives on a cliff's edge of obsolescence. The world is held together by a web of disposable objects. The only thing that reliably holds its value is the land on which it sits. Even when humans ravage it – often *because* humans ravage it – land never forgets its worth. It levels up even as it erodes. In California, land ages in reverse.

They say the only thing that would cool the housing market in LA is a catastrophe. An earthquake, a terrorist attack, or fires that rolled down from the canyons en masse and engulfed the city streets. But I wasn't sure I believed that anymore. The pandemic was a catastrophe that drove up real estate everywhere, especially the kind of real estate that comes with yards and trees. That's why the sleepy mountainside enclave in which I now paid rent had even higher home prices than the urban hipster neighborhoods I once inhabited. Not that I could afford to go back to those either. I am stuck in a catastrophe of my own making.

But the real disaster was eight miles away, laying in wait, almost obscene in its rawness, representing an actual problem for a change. The land was crippling me, but it was also the metaphor that kept me going. When the online world threatened to poison me, I could think of my land, the realest thing in my life, the albatross that embodied both my most distant dream and my most immediate problem. Every so often, I'd go to an open house on a Sunday, see the Teslas lined up on the street, each representing a buyer bidding over the asking price, and be reminded of the reason I dug this literal hole for myself. I couldn't handle the bidding wars. I wanted to be able to stake my claim and take my time. *Build your house, Meghan*. The experience would be terrible, yes. But at least it would be a new form of terrible.

'This may be a weird thing to do, but it's a very *me* thing to do,' I said to a friend on the day I closed escrow on the land purchase back in 2017.

That was both a true statement and the statement of an unfortunate truth. I have for some reason always seen my life as an exception to the rule. Not above the rules (God, no) but somehow adjacent to them. Ever since I saw the Werner Herzog film *Fitzcarraldo* in college, I don't think a week has gone by that I haven't had occasion to imagine myself as Klaus Kinsky hoisting that steamship over a mountain, a punk-rock Sisyphus. Given the choice between the smooth, straightforward way of doing something and the insane, convoluted way of doing it, I will choose the latter without a thought. It drives me and everyone around me crazy, but I always saw it as part of my charm.

I'm not sure how charming it is, really. You should always take risks in life, but the idea is that you balance them with lesser risks. For every crazy decision, you should make a couple of conservative ones. That's the part I missed. I bet the farm without even owning a horse. Or something like that. Maybe this analogy works better: I made crazy abstract paintings before learning to draw a straight line. And now the only thing I can think about are straight lines. A straight line out of this house project and into an actual house. A straight line through the rest of my life into whatever comes next. Having scarcely made a safe, normal choice in my entire life, I now want to make nothing but safe, normal choices until there are no choices left to make. But that would mean buying a reasonably priced condo, which I'll never do.

More than 200 days after putting it on the market, I managed to sell my land for $100,000 less than my initial asking price. If you added up the money I spent trying to develop the project over seven years, I probably lost at least $150,000. That those seven years coincided with the biggest runup in housing values in modern history is a wound I may never stop licking. When the deal finally closed, I was shaken and depleted. Friends I hadn't seen in a while still asked how the house was coming along, as though it was a relationship whose demise they hadn't gotten news of, and each time I was transported back to the early days of my divorce, when I'd have to shield my gaze from the pity on people's faces so as not to crumple under the weight of my own self-pity.

But now, curiously, I almost coveted pity. Instead of allaying their concerns with assurances that I was perfectly fine, I took a masochistic pleasure in relaying the extent of the damages. An innocent inquiry like 'How's your house coming along? Did you build it?' would be met with 'It was an act of spectacular hubris and a catastrophic failure. I lost more than $100,000 and I'll never own another home in California.'

To which they said the only thing there was to say: 'I'm so sorry.' Which was also the last thing I wanted to hear.

I wanted to hear that I was a wild adventurer, that the whole Sisyphean vibe was working for me, that $100,000 divided over seven years is less than $15,000 a year and, hey, many people spend that much taking drunken cruise vacations they barely remember? And I got to spend that money imagining my dream house and learning about zoning ordinances and minimum setback requirements and, hey, if that's not a life well-lived it's not *not* one either. Better to have loved and lost, etcetera.

But who was going to say that? I was a panic junkie begging for a fix. Catastrophe, catastrophe! The word formed a pleasing shape in my mouth. It soothed and punished at the same time. Upon the thud of my ego hitting some indiscernible bottom, I considered going to a 12-step meeting. But for what? Debting? Drinking? Gambling? Why is there no recovery program for real estate addiction?

Why am I even asking this question? This is the oldest story in my book. It is in fact the subject of an entire book that I wrote and published nearly twenty years ago: *Life Would Be Perfect If I Lived in That House.* That title captures the central delusion of my life. In the final pages, I wrote about my mother dying and I paid lip service to the idea that there are more important things than residing in a beautiful house. I did this to satisfy what was then an editorial requirement for memoir: the narrator must undergo a change. But I knew it was a lie. There is nothing more important than finding beauty in your home. My mother knew that better than anyone. She died in an apartment she loved, the winter sun streaming through the glass of the pre-war grid pane window of her living room.

I died a little on that piece of land the day I gave it up. That sounds dramatic because it was. It still is. Even now that I'm back to surfing the real estate listings (a largely hypothetical exercise, given the prices), my unbuilt house haunts me like a phantom limb. I don't want just any house. I want my house. My house was once inside of me, a roll of architectural blueprints I could hold in my hands even as the physical manifestation remained out of reach. It's now outside of me, an absurd entry on a Christmas wish list, a fantasy that gets more fantastical with every uptick in the interest rate. But still I search. I will never not be searching. The search is where I live. And there is beauty there, if you know where to look for it. I will never stop looking.

– The End Of The Personal –

August 2024

A nd so we enter the age of no reply.

A man applying for a position at a major corporation goes through twelve interviews over six months. He is given written tests and asked for labor-intensive work samples. He is asked about his salary requirements and willingness to relocate. He is told he is a finalist for this job and that a decision will be made soon. When the decision is made, the man only learns of it when he sees an ebullient social media announcement from the person who got the job. He never hears from the employer again.

A woman using dating apps goes on more than forty dates over eighteen months. No meaningful connections are made beyond an errant makeout session or a lackluster second or third date. At least half the men disappear without a word after the initial connection. Most of the rest are on the receiving end of her own disappearance. Everyone in this equation identifies as lonely. None can remember the last time they initiated a conversation with a stranger in real life.

An eight-year-old child growing up in an ordinary household on an ordinary street in an ordinary town can ride neither a bicycle nor climb on a piece of playground equipment without experiencing a paralyzing fear of falling off. Both activities require faith in the laws of physics he simply cannot muster, so he spends most of his time indoors. His parents feign dismay but each is secretly relieved at the chance to remove these sources of childhood peril from their list of worries. To save face, each accuses the other of being too coddling.

A writer who built her career by, as she describes it, 'bleeding onto the page' turns anemic and wan. For years, her stories were a miraculous gift, one she'd been given by some random force of nature and freely bestowed on the world despite being stingy in her other affairs. But at some point in the latter part of her early middle age, the stories lose their hold on her imagination. The life that for decades offered up one delicious anecdote after another now serves a cuisine she cannot fully taste. The act of writing, thus, begins to feel like describing the contents of a dimly lit room. There is something there, but it's not there *enough*. Whereas her best work once seemed to emerge from her veins, it now struggles to make its way past the gates of her brain.

Still, the writer searches for a vein. As the years march on, she taps and scratches and presses down on her skin. She turns her palms face up and holds her wrists under the light. There are physical veins present, more pronounced and protruding than ever, but they refuse to bleed stories onto the page. First, she thinks this is because her life, and therefore her stories, has become bloodless. She spends most of her time in front of a computer screen. The bulk of her communication is typed out on a keyboard or thumbled into a phone. She cannot remember the last time she walked down a city street unplugged from an electronic device pumping her with voices talking about politics or pointing out the idiocy of ideological opponents. She cannot remember the last time she was able to read more than twenty pages of a book without checking her email.

Her internal monologue, once a symphony of paragraphs and endless swirling sentences, is now a pastiche of memes and soundbites. Whereas her brain once incubated elaborate concepts and quirky, meandering theories intended for the page, she now thinks in shibboleths. She invents the word thumble to describe thumb-typing onto a keypad and experiences a momentary rush of pride at her new creation. If she has an interesting thought, she posts it on Twitter (or X, or whatever it's called now). She knows she has lowered the bar of her creative mind to nearly dystopian depths, but what can she do? Information now lives on tiny screens. Tiny screens are meant for memes and soundbites. Her sprawling paragraphs simply do not fit. Anything worth saying can be said in a three-sentence burst. If you think you need more than that, she tells herself, perhaps your message needs honing. Or perhaps you're in the wrong line of work.

Deep down the writer knows this is no excuse.

Nothing is stopping her from telling any story she wants. She just won't get read by as many people or get paid the way she used to, which if she were a real artist she wouldn't be so hung up about.

She decides then that it's not stories that have gone missing from her life but rather the abandon with which she was once able to tell them. And maybe this is not such a bad thing. On the page, she used to make a habit of gently ribbing friends, lovers, colleagues and random acquaintances in the service of expressing a 'larger truth' or even just getting a laugh. Now she knows that little good can come of that. She once believed in seeking ethical cover on the grounds that she was 'so much harder' on her own first-person self than on anyone else. But she always knew this was sham logic. The boss may forgo a salary and work on weekends, but she's still the boss. Joan Didion was correct when she said 'writers are always selling somebody out.' When the writer was young, she – like all young writers – kept this line in constant repeat in her head, telling herself that if Joan Didion could live with that kind of guilt so could she. But the writer now knows that such guilt is never really lived with as much as constantly tamped down like a rumor.

The writer has had to make a professional pivot. Her job is no longer just writing but 'content creation', which isn't so much a job as a skein of side hustles in which she communicates with an audience in one way or another, mostly by talking. One of the hustles is a podcast on which she analyzes and dissects the culture with a woman more than twenty years her junior. They're always on the lookout for material and when the writer spots a provocative, newly-published personal essay, she brings it up for discussion. Such essays tell of messy, complicated emotions around supposedly sacred subjects. They take a torch to sentimentality, asking if marriage and family is worth the trouble, if divorce is a privilege, if death can be a gift. They draw the map of the broken-in world.

The writer's podcast partner abhors these essays. She seem them as soiled laundry that happens to be made of words. She sees no difference between a memoirist who makes an honest and eloquent appraisal of her quirks and shortcomings and a reality television star or internet influencer who behaves grotesquely on camera. The writer finds this upsetting in a way she cannot articulate. Her partner has an uncommonly fierce intellect and is uniquely honest about the uncomfortable truths of the human condition. Yet she sees little value in giving personal voices to those truths, especially with a name attached. She thinks that if you must talk about resenting your children or hating your spouse you should confine it to Reddit forums or anonymous blog posts.

The writer tries to explain that wrestling with the complexities of your conscience and shaping them into an artful essay is worlds away from posting on anonymous forums or being an exhibitionist on camera. She tries to explain that art is the antidote to exhibition-ism. Her partner maintains that since most art is terri-ble (on this, the writer agrees) it would logically follow that art inherently lacks the power to override the scourge of cultural exhibitionism and 'garbage con-tent' more broadly. Besides, most personal essays are terrible (again, agreed) so why do them at all?

The listeners of the podcast, at least the ones who leave comments, are largely onboard for this analysis.

The writer built her career publishing essays like these. For them, she was both praised and pilloried and it was considered a mark of professionalism to take neither response very seriously. Her work was deemed sharp and audacious and also self-indulgent and solipsistic. Her prose was described as incandescent but also likened to drivel, which her detractors frequently miswrote as 'dribble'. Sometimes this hurt her feelings but usually she was so worn out from the rigorous editing process at the publications she wrote for that she was just happy to be paid.

The writer was known for chronicling her youthful antics. In truth, she didn't have all that many antics since she was usually at home writing, keeping herself out of trouble. But she learned to embellish things in such a way that every observation jotted into her notebook would add to her life a new layer of wonder. (If she dribbled out a publishable piece of writing in the process, all the better.) For many decades, this was a winning strategy. It paid her bills and earned her, if not fame, at least a notoriety that opened doors and drew people to her who would have otherwise never registered her presence. Editors rewarded her and students imitated her. Friends were cautiously amused (*I have to tell you what happened last night, but don't write about it!*) and romantic partners found themselves teetering between fear of exposure and fear of not mattering. *You're not going to write about me, are you? Why haven't you written about me yet?*

Over time, though, the writer began to suspect that building a career around personal essays was like sitting alone at a bar all night. When you're young and ripe on the vine, you can charm everyone around you. You can have them buying you drinks just to keep you on that bar stool, making them laugh and peppering them with questions that flatter them into delightfully shocking disclosure. (The writer knows a thing or two about this.)

But when you're old enough to be twice the bartender's age, you're a cautionary tale. People ignore you almost out of courtesy. If an older woman is drinking alone at a bar, people turn their heads as if granting privacy to a man urinating in a bush. In her rational mind, the writer knows this is a false analogy, but she can't shake the perception that the first-person genre is a young person's game. Writing about one's own life requires having enough self-awareness to say something valuable yet also enough naivete to think anyone wants to hear it.

The writer now sees that her fertility window for this kind of work lasted from approximately age twenty-seven to age forty-seven. During those years, she was frequently sent on trips for reporting assignments, speaking engagements or teaching gigs. This travel took her as far as China and Australia and on such trips she liked to eat dinner alone at the hotel bar with a couple of glasses of wine. Sometimes she chatted with the people around her and sometimes she pretended to read a book or a magazine while eavesdropping on the surrounding conversations. The whole experience was proof positive that things were working out for her; life was pretty damn great. Once she sat drinking in the enchanting upper deck cocktail lounge of a 747 en route from London to Johannesburg and thought that even if everything in her life started going downhill from here, even if the plane spontaneously broke into bits over the African skies, she had done alright for herself. She had arrived.

It never occurred to her that everything that arrives must depart. This never occurs to anyone.

In the last several years, the travel has all but stopped. The writer has also stopped drinking because she could no longer do so without getting a hangover and she was also drinking enough that she was hungover more days than not. Her head is clearer now, but the clearing is a stark prairie cut from what was once a lush forest. Time is marked by all that she does not do. She does not stay late at parties, knocking back the last of the cashews and having flirtatious arguments with pretentious men about pretentious subjects. She does not get romantically tangled up with pretentious men, or any men at all, really. She loves her friends ferociously, but her true kin are her boundaries. When asked to name two people she'd call in the middle of the night if she were having a crisis, she is stumped because she can't imagine calling anyone in the middle of the night for any reason.

In moments of crisis, the writer used to write. This was the emotional self-rescue of choice. It wasn't even a choice. It was a physical reflex, a form of breathing. For most of her life, there was no heartbreak she couldn't convert into poetry, no humiliation she couldn't reclaim as comedy. Though she can scarcely believe it now, the writer used to walk around in a near-constant state of amusement. From her early teens until easily her mid-thirties, her baseline visceral sensation was one of trying to stifle laughter in inappropriate situations. Her private mental jokes routinely had her bursting out in spontaneous giggles. In high school, she developed the habit of imagining that Woody Allen was seated in front of her in science class and forever turning around and cracking jokes that only the two of them could hear. The jokes made her laugh out loud like a crazy person. The teacher would be standing at the chalkboard explaining the difference between conductors and insulators and she would be trying to suppress her laughter at an invisible Woody Allen.

The writer now wonders if she could count on one hand the number of times she's burst into spontaneous laughter in the last several months, or even possibly a year. Regardless of the answer, it's a horrifying calculation. She runs this by a friend, whose response is that there's not much to find funny in the world anymore. That strikes her as a cop-out, but an alternative explanation eludes her. As an experiment, she tries to find the humor in everyday life. She studies the kink-inclusive dating app advertisements on the New York City subway and tries to see absurdist humor rather than pandering stupidity. She answers the spam call on her phone to see if any whimsy can be extracted from her interaction with the sad, poisonous scammer on the other side. At the supermarket checkout, she pictures Woody Allen standing in front of her in line making the Marshall McLuhan joke from *Annie Hall*, though she can't imagine what the setup would possibly be.

The thought of McLuhan brings to mind an afternoon in the early 1990s when she and a companion stood in an interminable line outside a New York City art house to see a screening of the documentary *Marshall McLuhan: The Medium is the Message*. The show was sold out and they didn't get in and she never actually saw the movie, though she spent the rest of her life making references to McLuhan as if she had. Around that same time, she also remembers standing in line outside the Lincoln Plaza Cinema to see Woody Allen's film *Husbands and Wives* and there being such excitement in the crowd that when the theater doors finally opened, something close to a stampede ensued. Many of her memories of early adulthood involve standing outside movie theaters, often with pretentious men whose jokes made her laugh.

Today, the writer no longer goes to the movies. She consumes content. She follows 'creators' who post videos on YouTube and TikTok. She watches troubled young people sitting in cars delivering tearful monologues into their iPhones. She watches teenagers in messy bedrooms prattling into the camera for hours or even silently playing video games while the world supposedly watches. Decades earlier, these teenagers would have lain on their beds, the phone cord curled around them like a lover, talking to their friends for hours and hours about nothing. Their parents would have yelled at them for tying up the line. If they refused to get off the phone, their mothers would have picked up the other extension and listened in until they did.

Today, those parents might have YouTube channels or Instagram accounts devoted to showcasing the aesthetic perfection of their home and families. They might publish essays about dabbling in polyamory or letting go of their cis-heteronormativity or learning not to kink-shame themselves. They might sit in their cars making tearful videos about how they never imagined life would turn out like this. By 'like this' they might mean any of a million different things. But most of them mean one thing, which is that even though objec-

166

tively speaking this is the best time to be alive in the history of human civilization, it somehow feels like the worst. Or at least definitely not the best.

The writer, herself a 'creator', follows along in fascination. This is where personal stories live now; on screen, sometimes in text form but just as often on video. Every day, millions of hours of content are posted by every sort of creator talking about every possible thing. They describe their divorces, diseases, heartbreaks, bankruptcies and addictions. They complain about being ghosted on the dating market and the job market. They share their conspiracy theories, their greatest hopes, their darkest secrets, their worst plastic surgery results and all manner of 'healing journeys'. Anonymous fans funnel into live streams like guests arriving at a party. The fans chat amongst themselves and poke gentle, or sometimes not so gentle, fun at the creators, occasionally issuing them funds as if throwing bills against the velvet linking of a busker's instrument case.

The writer searches and searches for the vein. Even as her physical veins grow yet more visible on her aging hands, the storytelling vein is a no-show. How can this be? The writer's job is to use the written word to make sense of the world and now she is unable to do this job. Content creation brings satisfaction and occasionally even pleasure, but it's not what she was put on earth to do and she feels she is falling down on her life's work.

When the writer was young, she had teachers who explained that making art is about making choices. Writing is less about the words you select than the words you're willing to leave out. She was taught that the personal essay was an exercise in the curation of details, that raw material was just the starting point. But somewhere along the line, raw material has become lived experience, which has in turn become the whole point, the entire game. The only reliable stories are those that read as if transcribed directly from a therapy session, or spoken into an iPhone camera.

Curation, for its part, is no longer a matter of choosing this word over that. It is not an element of craft or style. It is a means of managing personal reputation through the careful selection of images. It is something social media influencers do extremely well and pornographers do even better. Artists, not so much. No one really knows what artists do anymore. Least of all the artists themselves.

She wonders if the problem is that nothing in personal writing is ever left out. Even as news and information are cleaved into thinner and thinner slices of partial truths and glaring omissions, personal stories get less mysterious every day. Whereas she once strived for intimacy with the reader, she now imagines her work being received as a kind of assault.

The era of the personal is over. The writer sees this now. One day, she just gets it. Everything is personal so nothing is personal. The erosion has been a long time coming. First, the personal became political. Then it became porn. Now it has become dust.

It's not just a matter of chatbots and auto-replies and AI-assisted everything, though there is a lot that is the matter with that. It's that there is nothing she could write that would surprise anyone. When she started, it only took a few pungent details to knock a reader ever so slightly off her axis. It only took a few original insights to make a reader say *I never thought of it that way before*. Now, everything has already been thought of. There is nothing left to say. We have entered the post-personal age.

In time, the writer will give up her search for that particular vein and make do with other veins. The man who was ghosted on the job market will find resources he never knew he had. The woman who was ghosted on the dating apps will find love somewhere else entirely. The child who feared the playground will grow up unafraid of the ghosts in the machine that haunt his elders. His reading comprehension will favor words and phrases over paragraphs and pages. He will be able to put on a virtual reality headset and enter other dimensions of consciousness. He will be able to customize this experience to his own tastes and interests, yet he will not see these as personal choices as much as physical reflexes, a form of breathing. He will experience love and desire and disappointment and joy in the real world, but unlike the writer he won't be under the illusion that he has anything original to say about it. And for that, he might enjoy these experiences all the more.

The writer will be grateful to have lived and worked in the era that she did. She caught the tail end of the personal age and squeezed out every last drop. She even stayed past closing time. The pages of this book exist in spite of themselves. And in spite of herself, the writer will keep writing. Her personal stories won't come as easily or as often, but they'll always be lying in wait. *Why haven't you written about me yet?* She has never had the heart to leave that call un-answered.

— ACKNOWLEDGMENTS —

Many of these essays are the fruits of my stint at the Medium publication GEN, where I had the good fortune to be edited by Brendan Vaughan, Aaron Gell and Garance Franke-Ruta. I'm grateful for their wisdom, intellect and old-school rigor. At Notting Hill Editions, where I'm delighted the essays found a permanent home, I'm grateful to Jess Porter, Tom Etherington, and, above all, Rosalind Porter, whose patience, insight, and good taste are rare gifts in these times.

Concurrent to writing the material in this book, I was working on a somewhat embarrassing number of other projects. None would be possible without the support of more people than I could name here, but I'll take a shot at the highlights: Kathleen Sykes, my communications whisperer/executive super-assistant, is spectacularly good at the things the things I'm bad at – and a gorgeous writer on top of it all. Rina Bander answers my copyediting calls at all hours of the night and keeps me looking presentable on Substack, where my readers and supporters keep me fed. Michael Melcher has been an invaluable source of wisdom and practical advice.

On the podcast front, I want to thank my production team Diego Manzano and David Perez, my O.G. graphic artist-in-residence Scott Shaffer and my favorite sparring partner Sarah Haider. On the crazy-idea-that-just-might-work front, I am indebted to Robin Cressman, who devoted countless hours and boundless energy to helping build The Unspeakeasy from the ground up. I'm also grateful for the support of Kelly Griego, Luba Kaplanskaya, Elisabeth Mannschott, Robin McDuff, Deborah Robinson, Caeli Woflson Widger, and the hundreds of women who've set out with me on this unlikely adventure.

For creative inspiration and constructive commiseration, my friendship well runs deep. Alana Ain, Ingrid Abrash, Ellie Avishai, Leslie Bienen, Amy Correia, Lisa Selin Davis, Jody Gelb, Cathi Hanauer, Sarah Hepola, Anna Monardo, Michelle Pollino, Todd Sabel, Paul Shirley, Joan Wilson and Sarah Wolf: I'm so lucky to know you.

Finally, I'm grateful to my writing students, whose dreams and hard work are proof that it's not all a catastrophe.